D0726112

Justification
By Faith

Other books by Alister McGrath:

Explaining Your Faith, Zondervan, 1989

The Intellectual Origins of the European Reformation, Basil Blackwood, 1988

Iustitia Dei: A History of the Christian Doctrine of Justification 2 vols., Cambridge University Press, 1986

Luther's Theology of the Cross, Basil Blackwell, 1985

The Making of Modern German Christology: From the Enlightenment to Pannenberg, Basil Blackwell, 1988

The Mystery of the Cross, Zondervan, 1988

Reformation Thought, Basil Blackwell, 1988

The Sunnier Side of Doubt, Zondervan, 1990

Understanding Jesus: Who Jesus Christ Is and Why He Matters, Zondervan, 1987

Understanding the Trinity, Zondervan, 1988

ALISTER E. McGRATH

Justification By Faith

Academie Books Grand Rapids, Michigan
Zondervan Publishing House

JUSTIFICATION BY FAITH
Copyright © 1988 by Alister E. McGrath
First paperback edition 1990

ACADEMIE BOOKS is an imprint of Zondervan Publishing House,
1415 Lake Drive, S.E., Grand Rapids, Michigan 49506.

Library of Congress Cataloging in Publication Data

McGrath, Alister E., 1953
    Justification by faith : What it means for us today / Alister
McGrath.
        p.   cm.
    Bibliography: p.
    Includes index.
    ISBN 0-310-21140-9   ISBN 0-310-21141-7 (Paper)
    1. Justification.   I. Title.
    BT764.2.M44 1988
    234'.7–dc 19   87-36854
                                         CIP

Printed in the United States of America

90 91 92 93 94 / CH / 10 9 8 7 6 5 4 3 2 1

CONTENTS

PREFACE

For the Reformers of the sixteenth century, the doctrine of justification by faith was the center of the Christian faith, the foundation of their program of reform and renewal. The doctrine was no innovation introduced by the Reformers but a call to renovation, a call to grasp and proclaim the gospel of grace, to restore to the church the theological basis of her mission to the world. I hope that this introductory book will help a new generation of readers wrestle with the ideas that so stirred individuals such as Paul and Luther, in order that they may grasp and proclaim to a disbelieving world the astonishing and thrilling truth of what God has done for us through the death and resurrection of Jesus Christ.

Like every primer, this book makes no claim to be exhaustive or definitive but merely aims to guide the reader through a series of complex biblical, historical, and theological questions that are an inevitable part of the study of the doctrine of justification by faith. It will be clear that this little book is not intended as a substitute for serious study of the major works on the subject. I hope, however, further study will be made easier and more fruitful by this introduction to the themes and problems associated with the doctrine.

The work falls into two main parts. After an introduction, the first part deals with the biblical and historical background of the doctrine. The second part considers the contemporary relevance of the doctrine and in particular deals with the suggestion that the doctrine is out of date and irrelevant in the modern period. It is hoped that the reader will be stimulated to develop these ideas in his or her own thinking and personal ministry. An appendix deals with the difficult question of the theological significance of the doctrine, assessing its place within systematic theology as a whole.

Finally, the reader has a right to know why this book was

written. Some ten years ago, I began work on a study of the development of the doctrine of justification.[1] As I worked on that study, I began to realize how important the ideas in question are and how vital the doctrine of justification is to the life of the Christian church and the believer. I therefore decided that I would, as soon as I had time, attempt to explain and defend these ideas in a day and age when the doctrine of justification is often treated as a relic of a bygone age.[2] This book is the result, and any shortcomings it may have are a reflection on my weakness as an author rather than on my subject. For there can be no greater subject than what God has done for us in Jesus Christ and how this may be actualized in a new relationship in which he and we are together—a relationship that not even death itself can destroy.

Alister McGrath

1 INTRODUCTION

Contemporary theologians generally tend to treat the doctrine of justification as some sort of theological dinosaur—something that was of great importance in its own day and age but has now become extinct as a burning theological issue. They see it as something that survives only in fossil form, embodied in confessional documents dating from the sixteenth century but without contemporary relevance. One modern theologian who adopts this negative attitude is Paul Tillich:

> Protestantism was born out of the struggle for the doctrine of justification by faith. This doctrine is strange to the man of today, and even to Protestant people in the churches; indeed, as I have over and over again had the opportunity to learn, it is so strange to the modern man that there is scarcely any way of making it intelligible to him.[1]

But is Tillich really right? Is not what Tillich is describing simply the failure of theologians to *explain* what the doctrine of justification by faith really means? It is certainly true that the term "justification" today is more associated with word processing than with our relationship with God. But to say that "justification" seems strange as a theological idea to many today is certainly not equivalent to saying that the *truths and insights* which the doctrine of justification by faith expresses are strange or incomprehensible. It is the responsibility of theologians, who know what the doctrine means, to translate its significance into terms their readers and hearers may understand. The wise words of C. S. Lewis express this point perfectly:

We must learn the language of our audience. And let me say at the outset that it is no use laying down *a priori* what the "plain man" does or does not understand. You have to find out by experience . . . . You must translate every bit of your theology into the vernacular. This is very troublesome . . . but it is essential. It is also of the greatest service to your own thought. I have come to the conclusion that if you cannot translate your own thoughts into uneducated language, then your thoughts are confused. Power to translate is the test of having really understood your own meaning.[2]

If the doctrine of justification by faith is "unintelligible," it is because we have made it so and have failed to *explain* its power and relevance for the human situation. The failure lies with us, and not with the doctrine.

This book is intended to be an introduction to this central and neglected doctrine of the Christian faith. There is much that the reader needs to know about it—what its background in Scripture is, how it has been understood in the history of the Christian church, and what was at stake in the Reformation controversies over the matter. But above all, the reader needs to be stimulated to translate the insights of this doctrine into the language of a world which, we are told, has "come of age."

One of the reasons why the doctrine of justification by faith has lost its impact is the tendency of preachers to discuss the doctrine in general terms or in terms appropriate to a bygone age—without addressing it to the specific situation of their audience. Because it was in the sixteenth century, in the period of the Reformation, that the doctrine assumed prominence, preachers have all too often proclaimed the great theme of justification in terms drawn from the sixteenth century, fondly imagining that this is the *only* way of approaching it and that the doctrine must be taught and proclaimed in precisely this form! But, as the history of Christian thought shows, generations of theologians constantly have sought to apply the theme of justification by faith creatively to their own day and age. They were aware that their interpretation of the theme might not have cut much ice several centuries earlier and would do so even less several centuries later. They knew, however, that their task was to proclaim this great theme to their hearers *in terms they could understand*. We all too easily assume that the theme of justification was preached in exactly the same way from the first through the nineteenth centuries, only to fail us in the twentieth. But the truth is that the preachers of every age recognized the need to apply the theme to their specific situation—with the apparent exception of the modern period. For Augustine, the theme was to be proclaimed in neo-Platonist terms; for Anselm of Canterbury, in feudal terms; for Thomas Aquinas, in Aristotelian terms; for Calvin, in legal terms—in short, they proclaimed the doctrine in terms that drew upon the experience, hopes, and fears of their own day and age.

The theme of "justification by faith" is the fulfillment of human existence through the removal of the barriers that get placed in its path. To the individual who is preoccupied with guilt and knows that he cannot draw near to a holy and righteous God, the word of forgiveness is spoken: through your faith in the death of Jesus Christ and his resurrection from the dead your sins are forgiven—rise, a forgiven sinner, and go forward into life in fellowship with your God! To the individual who is overwhelmed by a fear of death, the gospel speaks the word of life: he who raised Christ Jesus from the dead will do the same for you—rejoice in that victory over death which is ours through Jesus Christ! In short, there is a need to particularize the theme of justification in terms of the specific situation of those to whom it is proclaimed. The gospel "sameness" is not being eroded by doing so—we are merely drawing on the fullness of its remarkable resources.

But this is precisely the problem—the fullness of those resources has *not* been fully drawn upon. The doctrine of justification, if it is to regain the place it rightly should hold, must be treated for what it is and not as a museum piece or as a fossil from the past that must be preserved in exactly the same form it had in the fourth, eleventh, or sixteenth century. It must be liberated from this prison and allowed to confront with its full force the expectations, hopes, and fears of the modern period. The church cannot be kept in bondage to the forms of theological expression used in the sixteenth century! Christian theology is concerned with the application of the history of redemption, which culminates in the death and resurrection of Jesus Christ, to the situation of the moment. It was this application that Augustine attempted in his day and age, and Luther and Calvin in theirs. And now, in turn, it is we who have to link the two horizons of the witness to God's redeeming actions recorded in Scripture on the one hand and the specific context of our own situation on the other.

If twentieth-century Westerners think of human destiny primarily in terms of ideas like "purpose," "existence," and "meaning," then the gospel must be particularized in these terms. By doing this, these concerns may be directly addressed and thence transformed. To do this is not to capitulate or surrender to the preoccupations of modern humanity; it is rather to recognize that the gospel needs to be addressed to points of contact with human beings in each and every age if it is to gain a hold and transform them. It is to exploit a means by which authentically Christian insights may be established, not to endorse contemporary concerns. We cannot argue twentieth-century people back into a sixteenth-century way of thinking if we are to communicate the vital truths embodied in the theme of justification by faith! The gospel meets people right where they are in order to move them on from there—and we cannot dictate where they should start from; rather, we must simply meet them *where they already are*. This is an essential precondition for the reappropriation of the doctrine of justification by faith and its reinstatement where it rightly belongs.

Another stumbling block theologians have put in the way of recovering the vitality and relevance of this doctrine stems from a mixture of Cartesianism and Platonic idealism. This is the concept of a universal abstract truth that is valid for all people and for all time. For some theologians, the doctrine of justification embodies exactly this sort of universal abstract truth. But is this really right? Is it not actually the case that the doctrine of justification by faith points to a central theme of both the Old and New Testaments—namely, that God wants and intends the restoration of a lost world to himself and to its true nature and destiny by breaking down whatever barriers are placed between it and him, and that in Jesus Christ he actually makes this possible? What we are talking about here is the mediation and manifestation of God's determination to restore his lost world through Jesus Christ *from whatever specific historical forms the human predicament takes at any given moment in time.*

It may be that the lostness that is experienced in one moment in human history is that of being held captive in slavery in an alien land—in which case the theme of justification by faith points to God's gracious act of liberation in the Exodus. It may be that the lostness experienced at another moment in that history is a profound sense of guilt at moral inadequacy—in which case the same theme points to God's gracious act of a real and costly forgiveness through the cross of Christ, in which all is squarely faced and all is fairly forgiven. It may be that the lostness experienced at another time is a deep and genuine desire for meaningful and purposeful existence—and once more there is a need to *particularize* the gospel by demonstrating how such an authentic way of existing is made available as a gift through the death and resurrection of Jesus Christ. Like any good preacher, the theologian must know the hopes and fears of his audience if he is to ground the gospel in their experience in order to transform it.

A further point that must be made concerns the intimate relationship between *doctrine* and *experience*.[3] Doctrines are fundamentally concerned with experience rather than with abstract conceptual truths! In other words, doctrines are attempts to preserve something that is all too easily lost through misunderstanding, namely, an experience. To use a famous analogy that goes back to Augustine, doctrine is like a hedge that protects a field. The field is the richness of the Christian's redemptive encounter with the living God through Jesus Christ, here and now—and the doctrine is simply an attempt to ensure that this experience can be *verbalized*, put into words, so that it can be passed down from one generation to another. And yet what is passed down from one generation to another is not merely a doctrine, a formula, a form of words, but the living reality and the experience that lie behind them. The doctrine of justification by faith is concerned with the Christian's experience of a redemptive encounter with the living God. It affirms that this encounter really can and does

take place and attempts to explain how it may take place—
what it is that we must do if we are to have this experience. It
cannot adequately describe this experience any more than any
of us could put our experience of God into words, but it points
to the reality of the experience and describes how it may be
actualized.

Some famous words of T. S. Eliot should be remembered
here: "We had the experience, but missed the meaning, but
approach to the meaning restored the experience." In other
words, we need not only an encounter with God, we also need,
if this encounter and experience is to be passed down to our
children, an intellectual framework within which the redeeming and liberating encounter with and experience of the living
God takes place. The doctrine of justification establishes this
framework. But it is the *experience,* the *encounter,* rather than
this framework the preacher is primarily concerned with! It is
possible to misunderstand the doctrine of justification by faith
as simply an obscure verbal formula—when it is in fact
concerned with transmitting and preserving the experience of
an encounter with none other than the living God. The doctrine
expresses and conserves this experience and encounter, but it is
not identical with it. What the doctrine of justification by faith
offers is not truth concerning God but the possibility of
encountering God. The preacher must explain how that experience may be had and how it is grounded in the life of his
hearers.

The general principle at issue is that of *contextualization*—or,
to put it in plain English, of taking the trouble to think through
what the gospel proclamation might mean to the specific
situation faced by your hearers. The gospel is perfectly capable
of being accommodated within every human culture and every
human situation—even the situation faced by a "world come of
age." If the gospel does not speak to people today, the fault lies
not in the gospel but in ourselves. The New Testament bears
eloquent witness to the power and vividness of contemporary
images and analogies to convey the theme of justification by
faith—and places us under an obligation to do the same in our
own day and age. Paul felt free to "become all things to all men
so that by all possible means [he] might save some" (1 Cor.

9:19–23), in order that the power of the gospel might make its full impact felt in the specific and unique cultural context of each historical situation. While cultural matters are relativized by the gospel's absolute claims, these claims must still be communicated and articulated in and to those specific life situations and contexts.

How might this be done? In a later section of this book we shall be looking at several points of contact with modern Western thought that allow the doctrine of justification by faith to be grounded in our contemporary culture. The general principles of such a procedure are set out by David Shank, who provides the following analysis of some of the many dimensions of justification as they relate to a variety of felt needs and cultural themes.[4]

TABLE 1

Context of Experience	From	To	Through Jesus
Acceptance	Rejection	Acceptance	Love
Direction	to err about	to aim at	Call
Festival	Boredom	Joy	Feast-giver
Meaning	the absurd	the reasonable	Word
Liberation	Oppression	Liberation	Liberation
Becoming	Nobody	Somebody	Invitation
Fellowship	Solitude	Community	Presence

Here, the theme of justification by faith is stated in a number of specific forms, each of which may be grounded in a given cultural situation. For example, we are not acceptable—but God accepts us as we are and where we are, through Jesus Christ. We have no meaning—but we are given meaning as a free gift of God through Jesus Christ. And so forth. And it is the task of the preacher, the missionary, and the theologian to ground this doctrine in the situation of their hearers, to unpack the relevance of that affirmation, and apply it.

It is at this point that a further difficulty must be noted. It is a difficulty known already to most, yet all too often overlooked. This is the danger of using technical theological vocabulary without explaining what it means, often without attempting even to restate or rephrase it. One of the gentle ironies of much of the contemporary attempt to preach justification by faith is a failure to realize that, as used by Paul in the New Testament, the term and the cluster of ideas it embraced had a freshness, an immediacy, and a vividness that are missing today. That vividness must be resupplied and refreshed. An illustration may help bring out the problem and perhaps point to one way of dealing with it.

A friend of mine had been feeling tired and weak for some time and had gradually come to believe that this was normal for someone his age. However, something he had heard someone say had made him suspect that there was actually something wrong with him—that he wasn't meant to be this tired and low. So he went to see his doctor. The doctor examined him and told him that there was indeed something wrong with him. He used lots of complicated technical terms such as "metabolism" and "calcium deficiency" to describe the problem. He referred my friend to a medical textbook in which his condition was described. But it still didn't make much sense to my friend.

Eventually, he gave up trying to understand the doctor. "Look, doctor, you and I just seem to speak different languages! How about explaining this to me in plain English? Can you tell me what's wrong with me without all these technical words?" And so the doctor finally really *explained* his problem to him. He told him how the human body normally works efficiently, breaking down food in order to extract the energy from it and changing it into a form that can be used for everyday activities. To do this, however, it needs certain substances. If these substances aren't there, the body can't work efficiently, and tiredness and lethargy set in. My friend's problem was that he didn't have enough of these substances. My friend now finally *understood* what was wrong with him, and the doctor proceeded to treat the problem.

This story probably falls within the experience of most of us. All of us know the tendency of the medical profession to talk their own private language. They use words every medical practitioner understands yet only relatively few people outside the profession are familiar with. It is a highly specialized form of shorthand, which allows a lot to be said in a very few words to those who already know the language—but which needs to be *explained* to those not familiar with it. The fact that most of us can't understand it doesn't mean that it's not true—just that it needs to be explained, translated into plain English, with a few homely analogies to help bring out the meaning.

Of course, it's not just the medical profession that uses jargon in this way. Anyone who tries to read computer or automobile manuals knows how any area of life develops its own specialized language—including theology. The vocabulary of the Christian preacher and teacher is littered with technical terms such as "sin," "grace," and "justification"—all of which make perfect sense to those who know what they mean but are unintelligible to the rest of the world. There is a need for the preacher or teacher to explain what these terms mean; to use plain English to convey their sense; to find analogies and illustrations to bring out their force and relevance; to *contextualize* them, explaining what they mean in the specific case of the person we're talking to.

In dealing with the doctrine of "justification by faith" we are handling a technical term that has become unfamiliar to many of our hearers. This does not for one moment mean that the doctrine is irrelevant—it means that there is an urgent need that it be explained, interpreted, and illustrated to meet the needs of a new generation.

To continue with our medical analogy, we could begin to illustrate the relevance and meaning of the doctrine like this. The gospel declares that we are like ill people who need the attention of a doctor (Mark 2:17). This comes as news to many of us, who weren't aware that there was anything wrong with us in the first place! The "world come of age" is rather like my friend who was ill but refused to believe it. The gospel declares that the name of this illness is sin, something that threatens to wreck our full potential as human beings. It is like a deficiency—something is missing from our system and needs to be added if we are to be whole. It is like a short in a complex electronic circuit—it throws the whole equipment into confusion. It is like a bug in a computer program—it turns an intelligent operation into chaos. And as the symptoms of this illness—such as being lost in the world, a sense of being far from God, of meaninglessness and guilt—are explained, we begin to realize that it is our own situation that is being described. We realize that there is little point in tinkering with the symptoms of this illness—the important thing is to deal with the illness itself. It is the root cause that must be identified and dealt with. The gospel passes judgment on us in the same way as a medical practitioner gives a diagnosis—declaring that something *is* wrong, and identifying precisely what the nature of the problem is.

And it is at this point that the gospel can be recognized as good news. It affirms the reality of sin but also the power and purpose of God to deal with it. It affirms that our human nature has been wounded by sin, that something essential to its well-being is absent, that we have been invaded by some hostile force, just as the body may be invaded by a viral infection. It insists on the seriousness of the problem while declaring that something can be done to remedy the situation.

As a younger man, I spent two years at Cambridge University, carrying out theological research at St. John's College. One of my great delights was to visit the chapel of nearby Kings College, a magnificent building, famous for its choral tradition. One of the great attractions of the chapel was an Old Master—a beautiful painting at one end of the main chapel building. One day, a protester made some sort of political gesture and, to the horror of all watching, produced a knife and slashed the painting. Within a short time, a notice was placed alongside the ruined painting: "It is believed that this masterpiece can be restored." Much of the same is true of human nature, according to the gospel. Standing at the height of God's creation, human nature has been seriously wounded by sin—and the gospel declares that this, the masterpiece of God's creation, can be restored by its loving creator.

"Justification by faith" summarizes the glorious affirmation that God is able and willing to deal with sin. An illness which we ourselves could not cure (sin) has been diagnosed by God, and a cure (justification) is offered. The futility of half measures, such as merely relieving symptoms, is affirmed. And we, like the invalid at the pool of Bethesda, are given the privilege of accepting or rejecting the cure: "Do you want to get well?" (John 5:6). The theme of justification by faith, as we shall see, speaks of our restoration to wholeness, of the recapturing in the garden of Gethsemane of what was lost in the garden of Eden.

To realize the full power of this good news, we need to try to think ourselves into a situation like that described in Arthur Hailey's *Strong Medicine*. A young woman is dying in the hospital. The attending doctor does everything he can, but the illness is incurable. He knows that within a matter of hours his young patient will be dead, with devastating results for her family. With remarkable skill, the author builds up a picture of the hopelessness and helplessness of the situation. And then, unexpectedly, a drug is rushed in. It has just been developed, and no one is quite sure what its effects will be. As the medical staff watch anxiously, the drug is administered to the patient. Then suddenly, what all had been hoping for, but none dared believe, takes place—the patient rallies and then slowly but surely recovers.

In many ways, this story illuminates the thrilling dimension of the gospel proclamation of justification by faith. The human situation has been transformed through the death and resurrection of Jesus Christ. As the first-century writer Ignatius of Antioch declared, the gospel proclamation is like "the medicine of immortality." The hopelessness and helplessness of our weak and mortal natures, trapped in the rut that leads only to death and decay, is transformed. What we could not do for ourselves has been done for us—and done well. In the famous words of Martin Luther, "We are like ill people under the care of a physician—we are ill in fact, but healthy in hope." The same sense of excitement, of realization of hope, can be found in the famous old Christmas hymn of St. Germanus:

A great and mighty wonder!
A full and holy cure!

Part One

The Background of the Doctrine

2 THE BIBLICAL FOUNDATION

The primary source of both Christian faith and Christian theology is the Bible. Scripture witnesses to the self-revelation of God in human history, beginning with the call of Abraham, continuing through the call of Israel out of the land of Egypt, and culminating in the life, death, and resurrection of Jesus Christ. The central theme of Scripture could be said to be God's dealings with his people.

But how do we enter into a relationship with God? How are we distinguished from those outside this relationship? And what obligations does this relationship place upon us? Questions such as these are raised throughout the Old and New Testaments. In the present chapter we propose to identify some of the more important aspects of the scriptural witness to God's gracious dealings with his people, which converge in the doctrine of justification by faith.

Many operas open with an orchestral prelude or overture. The original reason for these introductions was that the audience tended to arrive late, and the overture allowed the action to be postponed for about ten minutes until everyone had arrived. However, by the nineteenth century the orchestral prelude to an opera was well established as an integral part of the work (and the audience now had to arrive on time!). The prelude introduces the musical themes that will dominate the remainder of the opera, allowing the audience to get used to them and recognize them when they occur. Richard Wagner's operas, such as *Lohengrin*, are excellent examples of this development. And in many ways it is helpful to regard the first eleven chapters of Genesis as a prelude, introducing the themes that will dominate the rest of Scripture—themes such as human sinfulness, the rebellion of humanity against God, the graciousness of God, and the covenant between God and man. The scene is set for the great drama of divine redemption that follows. And then the curtain rises upon human history to reveal God calling Abraham and promising to make him into a great people (Gen. 12:1–3). In effect, Abraham is called in order to reverse the sin of Adam. And the response to that promise is faith. This point is developed in a famous passage, referred to several times by Paul: Genesis 15:1–6.

In this passage, God promises Abraham a son and descendants who will outnumber the stars of heaven—and Abraham believes this seemingly impossible promise. "Abraham believed the Lord, and [the Lord] credited it to [Abraham] as righteousness" (Genesis 15:6). Here we encounter a central biblical theme of direct relevance to the doctrine of justification—the idea of *righteousness*. What does it mean? Clearly it does not mean that God considered Abraham's faith to be a moral virtue which he was under some kind of obligation to reward (after all, the promise had already been made!). The difficulty is that the Hebrew word which most English versions translate as "righteousness" has no exact English equivalent.[1] In modern Western thought, "righteousness" tends to be thought of in terms of absolute, impersonal standards of justice and morality, and it is important to realize that this is not what the Old Testament writers had in mind. In the Old Testament, righteousness is a *personal* concept: it is essentially the *fulfillment of the demands and obligations of a relationship between two persons*.[2] The Old Testament sees each individual as set within a complex network of relationships. For example, a given individual will as a father have a relationship to his children; as a husband, to his wife; as a citizen, to his king as well as to the poor and needy; as an employer, to his employees; and so on. Each of these relationships is governed by obligations on the part of both parties, and fulfillment of these obligations constitutes "righteousness."

The most important relationship, the relationship that underlies all others, is the covenant relationship between God and his people. And "righteousness" in the Old Testament most often refers to the fulfillment of the conditions of that all-important covenant. When God or man fulfills the conditions imposed upon them by that covenant relationship, then God or man is, according to the Old Testament, righteous.

This recognition of the covenantal framework within which the concept of "righteousness" is set also allows us to gain important understandings of related concepts—such as "sin." Just as "righteousness" is primarily concerned with faithfulness, so "sin" is primarily concerned with faithlessness. While the biblical concept of sin has many aspects that could rightly be described as forensic or legal (such as the ideas of "missing the mark" or "falling short of what is required"), the idea of the betrayal of a personal relationship is fundamental to a biblical understanding of sin. Sin is about failing to trust God, challenging his authority, or failing to take his promises seriously (see Ps. 106:24–27)—in short, a failure to trust in God. We shall return to this grounding of the concept of sin in a personal relationship in chapter 7.

With this point in mind, let us go back to Genesis 15:6. We can now see that the basic idea is that faith in God's promises is regarded as "righteousness"—in other words, Abraham's relationship with God is "right" when he puts his trust in God's promises. The righteousness that is demanded of Abraham is faith in the *faithfulness* of God. Similarly, the Old Testament prophets emphasize that the condition required of the people of Israel if the covenant with God is to continue is righteousness—not primarily *moral virtue*, but rather *faithfulness* to God. This point helps us understand why the prophets protest against Israel's flirtations with foreign gods as much as—if not more than!—against their moral shortcomings. To worship a foreign god is not so much an act of *immorality* as an act of *infidelity* that breaks a relationship of personal trust and mutual commitment between God and his people. The close connection between "righteousness" and "covenant" in the Old Testament is evident. Indeed, so close is the relationship that it might be suggested that for either God or an Israelite "to act righteously" is "to act in accordance with the covenant."

Let us now consider the Old Testament idea of *justification*. It is interesting to note that the abstract noun "justification" is not found in the Old Testament—the verb "to justify" is found instead. It is evident that justification is understood as something active rather than as some abstract idea. "Justifying" is something God *does*. It is something dynamic rather than static. The basic sense of the Old Testament idea of "justifying" is probably best expressed as "declaring to be within the covenant." Throughout the Old Testament we find witness to the divine desire to redeem sinful humanity by initiating actions directed towards this end. God brings individuals into a relationship with himself despite their unfitness. The calling of Israel illustrates this point: God declares that he chose Israel to be his unique and exclusive possession, not on account of her merit or greatness (Deut. 7:7; 9:4–6), but because of his own loving, saving initiative. Then as now, God chose what the world thought weak and foolish. Indeed, if the Old Testament is viewed from the standpoint of God's gracious activity towards sinful humanity, particularly as expressed in the covenant-relationship, the New Testament appears as its perfect fulfillment.

The New Testament bears witness to the belief of the first Christians that believers were "right with God" (perhaps the most helpful translation of the term "justified") because of the death and resurrection of Jesus Christ (see Rom. 3:24–26; 4:24–25; 1 Cor. 1:30; 6:11; 1 Peter 3:18; 1 Tim. 3:16). The conviction that God had dealt justly and properly with human sin—rather than just ignored it or treated it as insignificant—is evident, particularly in the Pauline writings. We could say that the New Testament understands justification to be based upon the objective foundation of the death and resurrection of Jesus Christ.

Occasionally the term "justification" also has a clearly *forensic* dimension in the New Testament, implying the image of a court of law. "Justification" then assumes the meaning "declared to be right, or in the right, before God as judge." The verdict in question is basically about the individual's *status before God*, rather than his or her *moral character or virtues*. The New Testament, particularly the Pauline writings, thus seems to take up the Old Testament concept of righteousness as right relationship, so that "justification" comes to have the root meaning "being in a right relation with God," or "being right with God." The New Testament understanding of justification has thus primarily to do with how human beings enter into a right relation with God—a point that can be brought out by translating the Greek verb *dikaioun*, which is usually rendered "to justify," as "to rectify," stressing the relational aspect.

The New Testament, of course, uses other ideas to develop what is to be understood by being "right with God." Being right with God involves the expiation of sin (Rom. 3:25), being reconciled to God (2 Cor. 5:18–20), being adopted (Rom. 8:15, 23; Gal. 4:5), being transformed (Rom. 12:20; 2 Cor. 3:18), being sacrificed or consecrated (1 Cor. 1:20, 30), and so forth. All these ideas give flesh to the framework established by the basic idea of being right with God. God's gift brings with it transformation—and recent New Testament scholarship has noted how the basic Pauline idea of "the righteousness of God" conveys both the notion of a *gift from God* and *the transforming power of God*.[3]

These insights have gone some way towards allowing us to appreciate the brilliance with which Paul developed the "righteousness" and "justification" language of the Old Testament in order to describe what Jesus Christ has achieved for sinful humanity through his cross and resurrection. Salvation is given to us as a gift, bringing with it the transformation of the individual. God's gracious justification of sinners is offered to all through faith in Jesus Christ, a justification accomplished once and for all through the death and resurrection of Jesus Christ. It is not simply a past or present event but embraces the future: the verdict to be pronounced on the last day is brought forward into the present, in that God declares in advance that those who believe in Jesus Christ are in the right. The believer is justified and may live at peace in Christ (Rom. 5:1), having in effect heard the judgment of God and his justifying word (Rom. 5:1–2; 8:28–37; Gal. 2:15–20).

Perhaps the most significant contribution of Paul to the New Testament understanding of justification by faith concerns the manner in which we are put in the right with God. For Paul, justification takes place by the grace of God, through faith, not through the law (Rom. 3:22–24; Gal. 2:21). Of particular importance in Paul's exposition of this crucial point is the story of Abraham, which he recounts in Galatians 3:1–4:31 and in Romans 4:1–25. For Paul, faith in Christ is a response to the gospel: it comes from hearing the gospel (Rom. 10:17; Gal. 3:2, 8) and results in obedience. Of particular interest, however, is Paul's understanding of the relation of Christian believers to the covenant made by God with Abraham, which we must explore further.

Earlier, we noted the importance of Genesis 15:6 for an understanding of the concept of "the righteousness of faith." Abraham trusted in the promises of God—and by doing so placed himself in a right relationship with God. To be "right with God" is to trust in his gracious promises and to act accordingly. The call of Abraham is a call to enter into a covenant relationship with God (Gen. 15:7–11 is a description of the ritual of covenant-making). The theme of the covenant between God and Abraham and his successors is further developed in Genesis 17, where circumcision is established as the "sign of the covenant" (signifying that the individual stands within the sphere of the redemptive promises of God) and the full extent of the scope of the covenant in time and space is indicated.

In taking up the theme of the calling of Abraham, Paul clearly regards the patriarch as exemplifying the right relationship of the individual to God: faith in the divine promises and faithfulness. But it also seems that Paul sees a far deeper meaning in the call of Abraham—the establishment of the covenant people of God, based on the gracious promises of God and human faith in them. "All people on earth will be blessed through you" (Gen. 12:3). While there will always be elements of "understanding" and "assent" in any Christian definition of faith, the element of "trust" (relationship!) must never be minimized. Faith is understood as a humble, obedient, and trusting response of the individual to the promises of God. Faith is, in its passivity, an active readiness to receive from God. Grace gives and faith receives. Put very simply, faith says "Amen!" to God. And Paul clearly envisages that anyone who stands in this relationship to God stands within the covenant established with Abraham. Justification is by grace through faith—in other words, it is God who graciously gives and we who trustingly receive.

This obviously raises the question of the general relationship between faith and the Old Testament law, as well as the more specific issue of the relationship between faith and works. Paul's polemic against "justification within the law" and "justification by works" appears to be aimed primarily against the Jewish claim that Jews, and Jews alone, may be justified. Paul's emphatic declarations that *all* have sinned and that the "righteousness of God has now been revealed *apart from the law*" (Rom. 3:21–23) are directed against any claim on the part of a Jew to have the exclusive privilege of standing within the covenant with Abraham, to the exclusion of Gentiles. The theme of a "national righteousness," or of the Old Testament law as a charter of Jewish national privilege, is certainly one of the things Paul argues against by his emphatic insistence that *obedience* to the Old Testament law establishes an individual's right to stand within the covenant with Abraham.[4] Romans is of central importance to Paul's argument in that he argues in this letter that being a Jew is neither necessary (Rom. 4:1–25) nor sufficient (9:1–33) for justification. The sole condition, open to all, is faith.

The Old Testament law defines the people of God, those who stand within the covenant made between God and Abraham—and Paul clearly understands that faith in Jesus Christ fulfills the Old Testament law and establishes the believer's claim to stand within that covenant. Thus when Paul speaks of the "law of faith" (Rom. 3:27), he indicates that Christian believers are actually the true people of God, standing within the same covenant defined by the Old Testament law—the covenant made with Abraham. And in Galatians Paul argues forcefully that converted Gentiles have no need to become circumcised, since they already stand within the covenant made with Abraham on account of their faith.

This is not to say, of course, that Paul's doctrine of justification by faith was only relevant when the influence of Judaizers, who wanted Gentile Christian believers to observe the Old Testament law, posed a serious threat to the early church. Every age has its spurious concepts of justification, inadequate or misleading ideas of what we must do if we are to be "right with God." Justification does not take place on the basis of human works, nor does man's justification excuse him from the subsequent performance of good works. The Pauline emphasis upon God's gracious activity and man's trusting passivity in justification transcends the controversies of the Jewish and Gentile Christians and has direct and immediate relevance to our own day and age.

Furthermore, Paul's appeal to the constancy and faithfulness of God to his covenant is of considerable importance. According to Paul, God's justification of humanity through faith demonstrates his faithfulness to the promises once made to Abraham and to the covenant pledged to Abraham, revealed to Moses, and finally sealed with the blood of Christ. The great theme of the saving purposes of God throughout human history is proclaimed by the doctrine of justification by faith. The death and resurrection of Jesus Christ and the mission of the Christian church are not to be seen as a departure from God's original intentions, but rather as their climax and culmination. The covenant made with Abraham is renewed and revitalized through the death and resurrection of Jesus Christ.

There is not enough space here even to sketch the importance of the doctrine of justification by faith in the remainder of the New Testament. There is, however, one passage that has occasionally been held to contradict Paul's doctrine of justification by faith. This is James 2:14–26, which argues that justification is not by faith alone but by works that make it complete. It has frequently been suggested, with excellent support, that James's views are not directed against Paul's doctrine of justification by faith but against a distortion or caricature of it—and indeed, there are points in Paul's letters which seem to indicate that he himself had to contend with just such a distortion (for example, Rom. 3:8; 6:1,15). "You see that a person is justified by what he does and not by faith alone" (James 2:24) might seem to contradict Paul's vigorous assertion that we "are justified by faith, and not by observing the law" (Rom. 3:28; Gal. 2:16). However, it is obvious that no such contradiction exists or was intended. By "faith," James explicitly means "acceptance of revelation without corresponding behavior" (James 2:19), a dead orthodoxy that bears no relation to Paul's concept of faith. For Paul, faith involves the reorientation of the individual towards obedience to Jesus Christ—note the important phrase "the obedience that comes from faith"

(Rom. 1:5) and the assertion that both the *faith* and the *obedience* of the Roman Christians were widely known (1:8; 16:19). Paul and James merely state in different ways, and with different emphases, the basic meaning of the doctrine of justification by faith: we are graciously offered our salvation as a gift, which we receive by faith, and which transforms our natures (Rom. 12:20; 2 Cor. 3:18) so that good works result.

Two famous slogans sum up these important insights. The first dates from the time of the Reformation: "Faith is pregnant with good works." In other words, the gift of faith contains within itself the seeds of our new nature and our new desire for obedience to God, both out of gratitude for what he has done for us and as a result of the changes that are brought about within us through the transformative nature of faith. The second dates from the new interest in Paul, particularly in Pauline ethics, evident in the present century: "Become what you are!" In other words, through justification we are made children of God—and we must learn to act accordingly. Through justification, we are refashioned after the image of God—and we must learn to show this in our lives. The basic idea is that justification involves a declaration of our new status and relationship with God—and we must learn to accept this new status and relationship and refashion our lives and attitudes accordingly. God's gift brings with it obligations, just as it brings with it the ability to meet them.

In this chapter, we have looked briefly at the main themes of the biblical understanding of justification by faith. We have noted the two crucial themes of grace and faith: on the one hand the completely unconditional, loving, and gracious promises of God directed towards us in his actions, beginning with the promises to Abraham and culminating in the death and resurrection of Jesus Christ; and on the other hand the need for us to receive and appropriate these promises, with empty, open, and trusting hands. We have seen the remarkable scope of these themes, embracing the saving purposes of God from the calling of Abraham onwards. In the calling of Abraham, in the calling of the people of Israel, and in the calling of the Christian church—in each of these we find the same two themes developed. We are what we are by the grace of God.

God chooses us without respect to our merits (and overlooking our obvious demerits!) in order that he may make of us what we ourselves could never achieve (1 Cor. 3:5; 4:7; Phil. 2:13). It is a deeply humbling and inspiring insight—and one that is all too easily forgotten. In the next chapter we shall consider the first major controversy in the church over this theme. Although the Pelagian controversy belongs to the distant past, the same ideas continue to threaten to this day the gospel of justification by grace through faith.

FOR FURTHER READING

E. R. Achtemeier. "Righteousness in the Old Testament." In *Interpreter's Dictionary of the Bible*. Nashville: Abingdon, 1962. 4:80–85.

C. Brown et al. "Righteousness, Justification." In *New International Dictionary of New Testament Theology*. Grand Rapids: Zondervan, 1976. 3:352–76. It has an excellent bibliography.

E. Käsemann. "The 'Righteousness of God' in Paul." In *New Testament Questions of Today*. Philadelphia: Fortress, 1969. 168–82.

————, *Commentary on Romans*. Grand Rapids: Eerdmans, 1980.

B. Przybylski. *Righteousness in Matthew and His World of Thought*. Cambridge: Cambridge University Press, 1980.

J. Reumann. *Righteousness in the New Testament*. Grand Rapids: Eerdmans, 1983.

K. Stendahl. "The Apostle Paul and the Introspective Conscience of the West." In *Paul among Jews and Gentiles*. Philadelphia: Fortress, 1976. 78–96.

J. A. Ziesler. *The Meaning of Righteousness in Paul*. Cambridge: Cambridge University Press, 1972.

3 AUGUSTINE AND THE PELAGIAN CONTROVERSY

In September 386, a clever young North African teacher of rhetoric had an experience that was to prove to be of momentous importance for the future development of Christianity in the Western world. Attracted to the Christian faith by the preaching of Bishop Ambrose of Milan, Augustine underwent a dramatic conversion experience. Having reached the age of thirty-two without satisfying his burning wish to know the truth, Augustine was agonizing over the great questions of human nature and destiny when he thought he heard some children nearby singing *Tolle, lege* ("take up and read"). Feeling that this was divine guidance, he took the book nearest to hand—Paul's letter to the Romans, as it happened—and read the fateful words "clothe yourselves with the Lord Jesus Christ" (Rom. 13:14). This was the final straw for Augustine, whose paganism had become increasingly difficult to maintain. As he later recalled, "A light of certainty entered my heart, and every shadow of doubt vanished."[1] From that moment on, Augustine dedicated his enormous intellectual abilities to the defense and consolidation of the Christian faith, writing with a style that was both passionate and intelligent, appealing to both heart and mind.

Augustine left Italy to return to North Africa and was made bishop of Hippo (in modern Algeria) in 395. The remaining thirty-five years of his life witnessed numerous controversies of major importance to the future of the Christian church in the West, and Augustine's contribution to the resolution of each of these was decisive. His careful exposition of the New Testament, particularly of the Pauline letters, gained him a reputation, which continues today, as the "second founder of the

Christian faith" (Jerome). The first four centuries of the Christian era had seen intensive discussion of the identity of Jesus Christ and the nature of God, while the doctrine of justification had remained largely unexplored.[2] The onset of the Pelagian controversy in the early fifth century forced urgent consideration of this question—and Augustine's carefully weighed statements on the relationship between nature and grace and on the human and divine roles in justification have come to be regarded as perhaps the most authentic and reliable exposition of the biblical insights on these questions. In this chapter we will consider the issues at stake in this important controversy and the shape of Augustine's highly influential doctrine of justification.

As with any historic theological debate, it is important to distinguish between the actual course of the debate and the issues involved. While the former is of interest primarily to the historian, the latter are of continuing relevance to the Christian church. The historical course of the Pelagian controversy centers on Pelagius, a British (probably Scottish) layman living in Rome in the early fifth century, who was distressed by the questionable moral character of some Roman Christians.[3] By this time Augustine had already developed an understanding of justification that was much closer to the Pauline concept than that of Augustine's predecessors; he laid considerable emphasis on the human inability to achieve justification and the need for divine grace. Augustine's consciousness of his total dependence on divine grace seemed outrageous to Pelagius, because it appeared to deny human responsibility and the need for human exertion to become holy. It is certainly true that some Christians at the time regarded Christianity as a convenient way of obtaining salvation in the next world without undue effort in this one! In order to give his campaign for moral reform a theological basis, however, Pelagius developed a theology of justification that is generally regarded as at least compromising, and almost certainly contradicting, the crucial insights of the doctrine of justification by faith.

We shall summarize the main points of the controversy under four headings: (1) the understanding of the "freedom of the will," (2) the understanding of sin, (3) the understanding of grace, and (4) the understanding of the grounds of justification.

1. The Understanding of the "Freedom of the Will"

For Augustine, both the total sovereignty of God and genuine human responsibility and freedom must be upheld at one and the same time if justice is to be done to the richness and complexity of the biblical statements on the matter. To simplify the issue, denying either the sovereignty of God or human freedom is to seriously compromise the Christian understanding of the way in which God justifies man. Augustine in his own lifetime was obliged to deal with two heresies that simplified and compromised the gospel in this way. *Manichaeanism* (to which Augustine himself was initially attracted) was a form of fatalism that upheld the total sovereignty of God but denied human freedom, while *Pelagianism* upheld the total freedom of the human but denied the sovereignty of God. Before developing these points, it is necessary to make some observations concerning the term "free will."

The term "free will" (which is a translation of the Latin *liberum arbitrium*) is not a biblical term but derives from Stoicism. It was introduced into Western Christianity by the second-century theologian Tertullian, who borrowed this Latin term to translate the Greek word *autexousia*, which meant something rather different: "responsibility for one's own actions" is probably the most helpful translation. What Augustine had to do, therefore, was to keep the term "free will" (which during the two centuries since Tertullian had become so well established that its elimination was impossible) but to try and bring its meaning back into line with teaching of the New Testament, especially that of Paul.

Augustine says that the term *liberum arbitrium*, if it *must* be used, is not to be understood as meaning that human beings have complete freedom in every area of their existence. The basic elements of Augustine's teaching are the following:

1. We are responsible for our own actions, even after the Fall (notice how this goes back to the real meaning of the Greek

word *autexousia*, which Tertullian translated in such a poor way).

2. We are not puppets trapped in a web of fate, but we have real freedom of action in a number of spheres of our lives. It must be remembered that Augustine's opponents included the Manichaeans, who had a strongly fatalistic or deterministic outlook on life—everything happens through fate, and the individual has no control over things. Augustine insists that human beings have a real, if limited, freedom of choice.

3. This freedom is, however, compromised by sin, which biases our judgment to the extent that we are unable to break free from it. Like Paul, Augustine often regards sin as a power that needs to be broken—and sees the grace of God as the only way in which we can be liberated from its baleful influence.

Augustine developed a helpful analogy to explain the relationship between free will and sin. Consider a pair of scales, with two balance pans. One balance pan represents good and the other evil. If the pans are properly balanced, the arguments in favor of doing good or doing evil could be weighed and a proper conclusion drawn. The parallel with the human free will is obvious: we weigh up the arguments in favor of doing good and evil, and act accordingly. But what, asks Augustine, if the balance pans are loaded? What happens if someone puts several heavy weights in the balance pan on the side of evil? The scales will still work, but they are seriously biased towards making an evil decision. Augustine argues that this is exactly what has happened to humanity through sin. The human free will is biased towards evil. It really exists, and really can make decisions—just as the loaded scales still work. But instead of giving a balanced judgment, a serious bias exists towards evil.

Of course, critics of Augustine's theology of grace have pointed out that there are several logical flaws in his scheme. Augustine, however, was not concerned with logical rigor—his prime concern was to do justice on the one hand to the clear teaching of the New Testament concerning human bondage to sin and, on the other, to the human experience of being trapped by evil. While Pelagianism was admirably logical and consistent, it bore little relation to the teaching of the New Testament or to human experience. For Augustine, theology was not a matter of logical explanation; rather, it was about wrestling with the mystery of the nature and character of God—something that defies the neat categories of human logic and cannot be allowed to be subordinated to it.

Augustine thus argues that the human free will really exists in sinners, but that it is compromised by sin. Indeed, the human free will is so seriously compromised by sin that it is incapable of wanting to come to God. How then, he asks, can we ever come to God? And so Augustine develops the crucial insight that the grace of God is both necessary and sufficient to overcome the negative influence of sin. Two main images are used to explain how this happens.

First, grace is understood as the *liberator* of human nature. Augustine uses the term "the captive free will" (*liberum arbitrium captivatum*) to describe the free will that is so heavily influenced by sin and argues that grace is able to liberate the human free will from this bias and make it the "liberated free will" (*liberum arbitrium liberatum*). As we suggested above, sin is seen as a hostile power within us, which is fought and gradually overwhelmed by grace. To go back to the scales analogy, grace removes the weights loading the scales towards evil and allows us to recognize the full weight of the case for choosing God. Thus Augustine is able to argue that grace, far from abolishing or compromising the human free will, actually establishes it!

Second, grace is understood as the *healer* of human nature. One of Augustine's favorite analogies for the church is that of a hospital full of sick people. Christians are those who recognize that they are ill and seek the assistance of a physician, in order that they may be healed. Thus Augustine appeals to the parable of the good Samaritan (Luke 10:30–34) and suggests that human nature is like the man who was left for dead by the roadside, until he was rescued and healed by the Samaritan (who represents Christ as redeemer, according to Augustine). On the basis of illustrations such as these, Augustine argues that the human free will is unhealthy and needs healing. Again, grace is understood as establishing, rather than destroying, human free will, as the obstacles that prevent the free will from functioning properly are removed. Our eyes are blind and cannot see God—grace heals them in order that we may see

him. Our ears are deaf to the gracious calling of the Lord—until
grace heals them.

One of the more persuasive features of Augustine's account
of the influence of sin upon the human free will is its
faithfulness to our experience. All of us have experienced being
torn between *knowing* that something is good and *not being
willing* to do it. It is this tension that Paul recognizes: "What I
do is not the good I want to do; no, the evil I do not want to
do—this is what I keep on doing!" (Rom. 7:19). Augustine's
own prayer before his conversion also reveals this tension:
"Give me chastity and continence—but not yet!" This inbuilt
human tendency to want to do what is wrong—with such
profound theological consequences!—is well summarized in
the story about a visitor to a European monastery. This visitor
was shown to his room and told that he could do anything he
liked—provided he didn't look out of one of the windows.
Unable to control his curiosity, he eventually gave in to the
desire to find out what was so wrong about looking out of this
window—and was horrified to find all the monks there,
waiting for him! "They always look out!" was their final word.
This little story illustrates the profound tension arising from a
divided human will, which defies the neat classification of the
Pelagian system. In fact, many Pelagian writers recognized that
individuals are easily trapped by evil—and found this very
difficult to reconcile with their dogmatic assumption of the total
autonomy and freedom of human beings.

For Augustine, then, sin traps humanity within the sphere of
nature. It allows us freedom within this sphere of activity—but
it prevents us from breaking free from this sphere to encounter
and respond to the living God. Through grace, God enables us
to break free from the limitations of our natural condition and
to recognize and respond to his gracious call. For Augustine,
we are blind to God and our eyes must be opened by grace; we
are deaf to his word, and our ears must be opened in the same
way.

According to Pelagius and his followers, however, humanity
possesses total freedom of the will and is totally responsible for
its own sins. Human nature is essentially free and not
compromised or incapacitated by some mysterious weakness.
According to Pelagius, any imperfection in man would reflect

negatively upon the goodness of God. For God to intervene in any direct way to influence human decisions is equivalent to compromising human integrity. Going back to the analogy of the scales, the Pelagians argued that the human free will is like a pair of balance pans in perfect equilibrium, not subject to any bias whatsoever. There is no need for divine grace in the sense understood by Augustine (although Pelagius did have a quite distinct concept of grace, as we shall see later). In many ways, Pelagius resembles the subject of William Ernest Henley's poem "Invictus," a favorite with the Victorians:

> It matters not how strait the gate,
> How charged with punishment the scroll,
> I am the master of my fate:
> I am the captain of my soul!

In 413 Pelagius wrote a lengthy letter to Demetrias, a woman who had just decided to turn her back on wealth in order to become a nun. In this letter, Pelagius spelled out with remorseless logic the consequences of his views on human free will. God has made humanity and knows precisely what it is capable of doing. Hence all the commands given to us are capable of being obeyed and are meant to be obeyed. It is no excuse to argue that human frailty prevents them from being fulfilled—God has made human nature and only demands of it what he knows it can achieve. Human perfection is possible, and Pelagius thus makes the uncompromising assertion that "since perfection is possible for humanity, it is obligatory." The moral rigorism of this position, and its unrealistic understanding of human nature, served only to strengthen Augustine's hand as he developed the rival view of a tender and kindly God attempting to heal and restore wounded human nature.

2. The Understanding of Sin

For Augustine, humanity is universally affected by sin as a consequence of the Fall. The human mind has become darkened and weakened by sin and is unable to recognize God for what he is or to discern his glory. Sin makes it impossible for the sinner to think clearly, and especially to understand higher spiritual truths and ideas. Similarly, as we have seen, the human will has been weakened (but not eliminated) by sin. For Augustine, the simple fact that we are sinners means that we are in the position of being seriously ill and unable to diagnose our own illness adequately—let alone cure it. It is through the grace of God alone that our illness (sin) is diagnosed and a cure (grace) made available.

The essential point Augustine makes is that we have no control over our sinfulness. It is something that contaminates our lives from birth and dominates our lives thereafter. We could say that Augustine sees human nature as having an inborn sinful disposition with an inherent bias towards acts of sinning. In other words, sin causes sins: the *state* of sinfulness causes *individual acts* of sin. Augustine develops this point with the help of three important analogies.

The first analogy treats sin as a *hereditary disease*, which is passed down from one generation to another. As we saw above, this disease weakens humanity and cannot be cured by human agency. Christ is thus the divine physician by whose "wounds we are healed" (Isa. 53:5), and salvation is understood in essentially sanative or medical terms. We are healed by the grace of God, so that our minds may recognize God and our wills may respond to him.

The second analogy treats sin as a *power* that holds us captive and from whose grip we are unable to break free by ourselves. The human free will is captivated by the power of sin and can only be liberated by grace. Christ is thus seen as the liberator, the source of the grace that breaks the power of sin.

The third analogy treats sin as essentially a judicial or forensic concept: *guilt*, which is passed down from one generation to another. This was a particularly helpful way of understanding sin in a society that placed a high value on law such as the later Roman Empire in which Augustine lived and worked. Christ thus comes to bring forgiveness and pardon.

These analogies of sin have, of course, been taken up and developed since Augustine. For example, consider the following lines in A. M. Toplady's famous hymn "Rock of Ages":

Let the water and the blood,
From thy riven side which flowed,

Be of sin the double cure,
Cleanse me from its guilt and power.

The "double cure" of sin refers to the need for sin to be forgiven and its power to be broken (note the appeal to the death of Christ as the source of this cure). Or consider the famous hymn by Charles Wesley, "O for a Thousand Tongues to Sing," which has the following profound verse:

He breaks the power of cancelled sin,
  He sets the prisoner free
His blood can make the foulest clean;
  His blood availed for me.

The reference to breaking the power of "cancelled sin" is particularly important, since it incorporates the idea of liberation and forgiveness: "cancelled sin" is basically *forgiven* sin.

Pelagius, however, understood sin very differently. The idea of a human disposition towards sin has no place in Pelagius' thought. For Pelagius, the human capacity for self-improvement could not be thought of as being compromised. It is always possible for an individual to discharge his obligations towards God and his neighbors, and failure to do so cannot be excused on any grounds. Sin is to be understood as an act committed wilfully against God. Pelagianism thus appears as a rigid form of moral authoritarianism—an insistence that humanity is under obligation to be sinless and an absolute rejection of any excuse for failure. Humanity is born sinless, and people only sin through deliberate actions (Pelagius insisted that many Old Testament figures actually remained sinless). Only those who were morally upright could, according to Pelagius, be allowed to enter the church—whereas Augustine, with his concept of fallen human nature, was happy to regard the church as a hospital where fallen humanity could recover and grow gradually in holiness through grace.

3. The Understanding of Grace

One of Augustine's favorite biblical texts is John 15:5, "Apart from me you can do nothing." He sees us as totally dependent upon God for our salvation, from the beginning to the end of our lives. Augustine draws a careful distinction between the *natural human faculties*—given to humanity as its natural endowment—and *additional and special gifts of grace*. God does not leave us where we are by nature, incapacitated by sin and unable to redeem ourselves, but he gives us his grace in order that we may be healed, forgiven, and restored. Augustine's view of human nature is that it is frail, weak, and lost, and needs divine assistance and care if it is to be restored and renewed. Grace, according to Augustine, is God's generous and quite unmerited attention to humanity by which this process of healing may begin. Human nature requires transformation through the grace of God, so generously given.

Pelagius uses the term "grace" in two different ways. First, grace is to be understood as the *natural human faculties*. For Pelagius, these are not corrupted or incapacitated or compromised in any way. They have been given to humanity by God, and they are meant to be used. When Pelagius asserts that humanity can, through grace, choose to be sinless, what he means is that the natural human faculties of reason and will should enable humanity to choose to avoid sin. As Augustine was quick to point out, of course, this is not what the New Testament understands by the term!

Second, Pelagius understands grace to be *external enlightenment* provided for humanity by God. Pelagius gives several examples of such enlightenment—for instance, the Ten Commandments and the moral example of Jesus Christ. Grace informs us what our moral duties are (otherwise, we would not know what they were), but it does not assist us in the performance of these duties. We are enabled to avoid sin through the teaching and example of Christ. But, as Augustine was quick to point out, "this locates the grace of God in the law and in teaching"—whereas what the New Testament envisages is grace as divine assistance to humanity, rather than just some sort of moral advice. For Pelagius, grace is *external and passive*, something outside us, whereas Augustine understands grace as the real and redeeming presence of God in Christ within us, transforming us—something *internal and active*.

According to Pelagius, then, God created humanity and provided information concerning what is right and what is wrong—and then ceased to take any interest in humanity, apart from the final day of judgment. On that day, individuals will be judged according to whether they have fulfilled *all* their moral obligations. Failure to have done so leads to eternal punishment—and Pelagius' exhortations to moral perfection are characterized by their emphasis upon the dreadful fate of those who fail in this matter. For Augustine, however, humanity was created good by God and then fell away from him—but God, in his grace, came (and comes) to rescue fallen humanity from its predicament. God assists us by healing us, enlightening us, strengthening us, and continually working within us in order to bring us back to him. For Pelagius, humanity merely needs to be shown what to do and can then be left to achieve it unaided; for Augustine, humanity needs to be shown what to do and then must be gently aided at every point if this objective is even to be approached, let alone fulfilled.

4. The Grounds of Justification

For Augustine, humanity is justified as an act of grace: even human good works are the result of God's working within fallen human nature. Everything leading up to salvation is the free and unmerited gift of God, given out of love for his people. All too often Augustine's views on grace are regarded as threatening—whereas they are in fact deeply reassuring! Weak and feeble though we are, and prone to sin, God is at work within us, achieving something we ourselves could never do. Through the death and resurrection of Jesus Christ, God is enabled to deal with fallen humanity in this remarkable and generous manner, giving us what we do not deserve (salvation), and withholding from us what we do deserve (condemnation).

Augustine's exposition of the parable of the laborers in the vineyard (Matt. 20:1–10) is of considerable importance in this respect. As we shall see, Pelagius argued that God rewards each individual strictly on the basis of merit, of the *work* which that individual has performed. Augustine, however, points out that this parable indicates that the basis of the reward given to the individual is the *promise made to* that individual. Augustine emphasizes that the laborers did not work for equal periods in the vineyard, yet the same wage (a denarius) was given to all. The owner of the vineyard had promised to pay each individual a denarius, provided that he worked from the time when he was called till sundown—even though this meant that some worked all day and others only for an hour. And so Augustine draws the important conclusion that the basis of our justification is the divine promise of grace made to us. God is faithful to his promises, and justifies sinners. Just as the laborers who began work in the vineyard late in the day had no claim to a full day's wages, except through the generous promise of the owner, so sinners have no claim to justification and eternal life, except through the gracious promises of God, received through faith.

For Pelagius, however, humanity is justified on the basis of its merits: human good works are the result of the exercise of the totally autonomous human free will, in fulfillment of an obligation laid down by God. A failure to meet this obligation opens the individual to the threat of eternal punishment. If an individual is to be justified, he must meet the full rigor of the demands God makes of him. Jesus Christ is involved in salvation only to the extent that he reveals, by his actions and teaching, exactly what God requires of the individual. If Pelagius can speak of "salvation in Christ" it is only in the sense of "salvation through imitating the example of Christ."

In comparing Augustine and Pelagius on these four points, the totally different perspectives of their understandings of the way in which God redeems humanity are obvious. Through the centuries, the church has always regarded Augustine as by far the more reliable exponent of Paul—which explains why Augustine is often referred to as "the doctor of grace" (*doctor gratiae*). Augustine's gospel is that of a gracious God passionately concerned for the salvation of sinful humanity. Pelagius' gospel initially seems to be sweet reasonableness itself but on closer inspection turns out to be a fanatical moral rigorism. Yet Pelagius' ideas are revived in every age of the church. Perhaps the most celebrated of these revivals is generally thought to have been the occasion for the movement that is the subject of the next chapter—the Reformation.

FOR FURTHER READING

For basic material, see:

Alister E. McGrath. *Iustitia Dei: A History of the Christian Doctrine of Justification*. 2 vols. Cambridge: Cambridge University Press, 1986. 1:17–36; 51–54; 71–75.

On Augustine, see further:

Gerald Bonner. *St. Augustine of Hippo: Life and Controversies*. Philadelphia: Westminster, 1963.

Peter Brown. *Augustine of Hippo: A Biography*. Berkeley: University of California Press, 1967.

On Pelagius, see further:

Robert F. Evans. *Pelagius: Inquiries and Reapprisals*. New York: Seabury, 1968.

4   THE REFORMATION

Although there was extensive discussion of the doctrine of justification during the Middle Ages, it is generally recognized that the doctrine proved to be of conclusive importance in the Reformation debates of the sixteenth century.[1] The present chapter will deal with the main contributions of those debates to our understanding of the doctrine. First, we must consider the views on justification that were in circulation in the Middle Ages.

Augustine died in 430, shortly before the barbarians invaded his city of Hippo in North Africa. Although they destroyed the city, they preserved Augustine's writings. It was almost as if they sensed that Western Christianity would need to rely upon his words as the ancient world died away and the Dark Ages were born. When the clouds of the Dark Ages began to lift from Europe in the eleventh century, it was to the writings of Augustine that medieval theologians turned for guidance and inspiration. The result was that all medieval theologians were influenced to a greater or lesser degree by Augustine, and all medieval theology may be thought of as "Augustinian" to at least some extent. However, as the fourteenth and fifteenth centuries dawned, it became increasingly clear that some of these medieval interpretations of Augustine were open to question.

By the late medieval period, all sorts of questionable popular practices had developed that reflected a lack of theological clarity. It was widely held that salvation was something that could be earned by good works, which included fulfilling the moral law and observing a vast range of ecclesiastical rules. The sale of indulgences—which so outraged Luther—shows that it was widely thought possible to avoid purgatory by paying the appropriate amount of money. The famous words of the indulgence dealer Johannes Tetzel sum up this attitude:

> As soon as the coin in the coffer rings
> The soul from purgatory springs!

For a substantial sum of money, it was possible for an individual to buy forgiveness for every sin committed in a lifetime and thus guarantee a direct entry into heaven. And so forgiveness of sins was treated as a marketable commodity. Although Augustine may have continued to influence at least some academic theologians, popular Pelagianism was rampant. For this reason, the Reformers recognized that it was necessary to rediscover both the academic and the pastoral elements of the doctrine of justification by faith—and the reform program associated with Martin Luther represents an attempt to do precisely this.

To begin with, we must understand that the late medieval church was seriously confused over the doctrine of justification. There was a bewildering variety of answers to the crucial question that was being asked by so many at the dawn of the sixteenth century: "What must I do to be saved?" Indeed, there was such confusion that the question simply could not be answered with any degree of confidence, as is reflected in Luther's early struggle with the problem of how he could find a gracious God.

To fully appreciate Luther, we need to understand his theological background. All of us know how "schools of thought" get established. Someone presents some exciting new ideas, and a group of followers builds up around him and develops his teachings. This happens in almost every area of human thought. Think of the influence of Sigmund Freud in the field of psychoanalysis, for example. A famous example in the area of theology is the development of Liberal Protestantism in Germany in the nineteenth century, based on the ideas of F. D. E. Schleiermacher and Albrecht Ritschl. But every now and then a thinker arises *within* an established school of thought who initially accepts its ideas and then comes to find them unacceptable. A good example from the present century is the great Swiss theologian Karl Barth. Initially Barth stood within the Liberal Protestant school—but on rethinking his ideas in the light of both Paul's Letter to the Romans and the First World War, he recognized that Liberal Protestantism was based on a totally inadequate view of God and of humanity. And so the "rediscovery of God"—which has had enormous influence on twentieth-century theology—began.

The latter is what took place in the case of Martin Luther, in the early sixteenth century. The theological school that became dominant in many northern European universities in the late fifteenth and early sixteenth centuries was the *via moderna* ("the modern way"), also known as "nominalism."[2] This school came to exercise considerable influence over many leading theologians of the late medieval period, including the young Luther, who studied at the University of Erfurt before entering the Augustinian monastery in the same town in 1505. Both university and monastery were dominated by the *via moderna*, and all the evidence available indicates that Luther followed the teaching of this school until the 1510s. After a period of study, teaching, and traveling, Luther became professor of biblical studies at the University of Wittenberg in 1512, where he delivered lectures on the Psalms (1513–15), Romans (1515–16), Galatians (1516–17), and Hebrews (1517–18). At some point during these lectures, Luther broke free from the theology of justification of the *via moderna* and forged his own reforming theology based on his new understanding of the doctrine of justification.

In view of the historical importance of the development of Luther's doctrine of justification, this chapter focuses on the two most common questions concerning Luther's break-through. First, what were Luther's original views on justification and in what way did they change? Second, when did this change take place?

Luther's early views on justification (up to about 1514) can be summarized as follows. God has entered into a covenant or contract (the Latin word *pactum* is used to express this idea) with humanity. This contract lays down certain conditions that must be met before it is possible to be justified.[3] God has promised that he will justify anyone who meets the precondition that the individual turn to God in faith and humility. Both faith and humility are human works, which the individual may achieve without the assistance of divine grace. Once this precondition has been met, God is under a self-imposed obligation (because of his promise) to justify the individual in question. God is gracious towards humanity in that he has established a framework within which an individual may be justified through a minimum effort. Nevertheless, a definite and specific human effort is required.

This brings us to the concept of the "righteousness of God," of such central importance to Luther's development. At this early stage, Luther understood the "righteousness of God" (*iustitia Dei*) to refer to an impersonal attribute of God, which stands over and against us and judges us with complete impartiality on the basis of whether or not we have met the basic precondition for justification. If we have, God's verdict is justification; if we have not, the verdict is condemnation. God is completely fair in his dealings with humanity: whoever meets the basic precondition of faith and humility has a right to demand justification on the basis of the divine promise to justify anyone who fulfills the precondition. The same demand is made under both the Old and New Testaments. For the theologians of the *via moderna*, it was unthinkable that God should give the sinner any special assistance in this matter—to do so would amount to favoritism. The same condition had to be met by everyone, without any divine aid. To Luther, and to many others at the time, this seemed remarkably like Pelagianism—the assertion that an individual could justify himself without divine grace. Indeed, one important work written in the fourteenth century against this theology of justification was entitled *The Cause of God against the Modern Pelagians*.

But what happens if it is impossible to meet this precondition through one's own efforts? The young Luther was intensely aware of his own sinfulness, and as time progressed became increasingly uncertain whether he could meet these demands. The demand for faith—which seemed so simple and easy— proved to be more than he thought he could fulfill and drove the young Luther to near-despair. The central question that burdened him was this: "How can I find a gracious God" (*Wie kriege ich einen gnädigen Gott?*). For Luther, the twin conditions of faith and humility made justification impossible: it was as if

God promised a blind man a million dollars, provided that man could see, or as if someone who could not speak was promised the contents of Fort Knox if he recited aloud the works of Shakespeare. The promise was real enough—but the conditions laid down made it impossible that it could ever be fulfilled. Luther became increasingly persuaded that an individual needed the assistance of the grace of God if justification was to be a real possibility.

Luther reflected constantly on Romans 1:17: "In the gospel a righteousness of God is revealed," but he could not see how the revelation of the "righteousness of God" was gospel, "good news." And then at some point—we are not exactly sure when—he seems to have had a breakthrough. Fortunately, we have his own account of what happened. In the final year of his life, Luther published a brief account of his theological reflections as a young man.[4] Luther recalls that he was taught to interpret the "righteousness of God" as that righteousness by which God himself is righteous and punishes sinners, so that the revelation of the "righteousness of God" in the gospel was nothing other than the revelation of the wrath of God directed against sinners. How could this be good news for *sinners*? Luther continues:

> At last, by the mercy of God, meditating day and night, I gave heed to the context of the words, namely "In it the righteousness of God is revealed," as it is written, "He who through faith is righteous shall live." There I began to understand that the righteousness of God is that by which the righteous lives by a gift of God, namely by faith. And this is the meaning: the righteousness of God is revealed by the gospel, namely the passive righteousness with which merciful God justifies us by faith, as it is written, "He who through faith is righteous shall live." Here I felt that I was altogether born again and had entered paradise through open gates.

This passage vibrates with the excitement of discovery as Luther relates how he came to realize that the righteousness of God that is revealed in the gospel is *a gift of God given to sinners.* The God who is revealed in the gospel is not a harsh judge who judges us on the basis of our merits, but a merciful and gracious

God who gives his children something they could never attain by their own unaided efforts.

What, then, did Luther come to understand by the "righteousness of God"? In a series of images, Luther builds up a picture of a righteousness, given to us by God, which remains outside us. Just as a mother hen covers her chicks with her wing, so God clothes us with an "alien righteousness." It is something that is given to us, something that we ourselves could never obtain. We stand as justified sinners before God, clothed with a righteousness that is not our own but is given to us by God himself. Our righteous standing with God, the fact that we are "right with God" through the faith he gives us, is ultimately due to the overwhelming grace of God rather than to our efforts to make ourselves righteous in his sight. The great theme of "justification by faith alone," so characteristic of Luther, extols the graciousness and generosity of God as much as it affirms the impotence of sinful humanity to justify itself. We are passive, and God is active, in our justification. Grace gives, and faith gratefully receives—and even that faith must itself be seen as a gracious gift of God. "Justification by faith" affirms that it is God who justifies us in an act of grace, by means of a gift which he himself gives us—faith. To suggest that Luther teaches that we are justified by a human work (faith) is to miss the entire point of his doctrine of justification. Even the faith through which we are justified is a gift of God!

Luther develops this understanding of the "righteousness of God" in terms of a "wonderful exchange" between Christ and the believer. Using the analogy of a human marriage, Luther argues that Christ and the believer are united through faith: Christ bestows his righteousness upon the believer, and the believer's sin is transferred to Christ. Luther thus speaks of "a grasping faith" (fides apprehensiva), a faith that grasps Christ and unites him to the individual believer, in order that this wonderful exchange of attributes may take place. Luther insists that justification involves a change in an individual's status before God, rather than a fundamental change in his nature: although the individual believer is righteous by faith, he remains a sinner. It is this insight that underlies Luther's famous assertion that the believer is "righteous and a sinner at one and the same time" (simul iustus et peccator).

In many ways, the Reformation may be regarded as a rediscovery of the Pauline writings, and especially of the doctrine of justification by grace through faith. Although the Reformation insights into justification are often summarized in the slogan "justification *sola fide*" (by faith alone), they are probably better represented in the slogan "justification *per fidem propter Christum*" (through faith on account of Christ). For the Reformers, our justification does not rest on anything we ourselves do, but rather on the work of Christ—we are justified when we receive this passively, through faith. Faith is the earthen vessel that conveys the treasure of Christ, as Calvin put it. God is active and we are passive in justification. Even the faith through which we believe and receive Christ is a work of God.

This point is of importance in connection with one of the leading features of Protestant spirituality—the concept of *assurance*. For Luther and Calvin alike, the question of how the believer can rest assured that he is justified was of central importance. The living of the Christian life, with all the ethical and spiritual consequences this entails, is dependent on the knowledge that this Christian life *really has been begun*. The believer is able to rest secure in the knowledge that he *has* been justified because justification does not depend on him in any way. It is God who establishes the basis of the Christian life, and the believer may build on this as he explores the ethical, political, and spiritual consequences of his new life in Christ. In short, the doctrine of justification by faith is a *security doctrine* for the Reformers—and the concept of forensic justification was seen as establishing the foundation of the Christian life far more reliably than the Augustinian concept of justification by infused, imparted, or inherent righteousness.

A popular misunderstanding of the Reformation doctrine of justification by faith is that we are justified *because we believe*, that it is our decision to believe that brings about our justification. Here faith is understood as a human work, something which we do—and so we are justified on the basis of our works! This is actually the later doctrine, especially associated with seventeenth-century Arminianism, of "justification *propter fidem per Christum*," justification on account of faith through Christ (rather than "justification *per fidem propter*

Christum," justification by faith on account of Christ). The
Reformation doctrine affirms the activity of God and the
passivity of humanity in justification. Faith is not something
human we do, but something divine that is wrought within us.
"Faith is the principal work of the Holy Spirit" (Calvin), and it
is through faith that Christ and all his benefits are received.
Calvin summarizes these benefits as "being reconciled to God
through Christ's sinlessness" and "being sanctified by the spirit
of Christ."

Perhaps one of the most famous passages in which this
recognition is described was written by John Wesley in his
journal entry for 24 May 1738. After a long period of wrestling
with the question how he could ever come to a living faith in
God, he describes how the realization that faith is something
God gives to us, rather than something we must achieve,
changed his outlook on existence:

> In the evening I went very unwillingly to a society in
> Aldersgate Street, where one was reading Luther's preface
> to the Epistle to the Romans. About a quarter before nine,
> while he was describing the change which God works in
> the heart through faith in Christ, I felt my heart strangely
> warmed. I felt that I did trust in Christ, Christ alone for
> salvation, and an assurance was given me that he had
> taken away my sins, even mine, and saved me from the
> law of sin and death.[5]

Luther's total emphasis on the gift-character of salvation led
him to call into question any theology that failed to do justice to
this aspect of the gospel. Initially, Luther seems to have
directed his criticisms chiefly against the theological school to
which he once belonged, the *via moderna*—but his conviction
that it was not just this theological school but the entire church
of his day that had fallen into the Pelagian heresy led him to
mount a campaign for doctrinal reform that would prove to be
unstoppable. The central theme of the Reformation—affirmed
in slogans such as *sola gratia, sola fide,* and *soli Christo*—was the
graciousness of God. For Luther, to compromise the gospel of
the grace of God was to destroy the central element of
Christianity. It is for this reason that Luther's views have been
summarized by designating the doctrine of justification by faith

as "the article by which the church stands or falls." In the Schmalkald Articles of 1535, Luther wrote thus of the doctrine of justification: "Nothing in this article may be given up or compromised. . . . On this article rests all that we teach and practice against the pope, the devil and the world." By compromising this central element of the gospel, the church had lost the right to call itself "the church of God"—and thus Luther felt justified in breaking away from this "church" in order to restore to it its theological basis. Thus it is important to notice that Luther did not criticize the church of his day on the basis of a direct *ecclesiological* argument (in other words, an argument about the nature of the church), but on the basis of his conviction that the church, by compromising the gospel of free grace, had fallen into the Pelagian heresy.

This conviction led to the German Reformation. Initially, it was restricted to the theology faculty at the University of Wittenberg, but by the 1520s it was enjoying considerable popular support. However, Luther was no systematic theologian; he preferred to write in response to particular needs, rather than writing theological textbooks, and the task of consolidating his doctrine of justification was left to others, most notably Philip Melanchthon, who was responsible for drawing up the famous Augsburg Confession of 1530. It seems that Luther's doctrine of justification was modified somewhat by his followers, such as Melanchthon,[6] and one aspect of this development needs to be noted carefully.

Earlier we noted Luther's idea of the "alien righteousness of Christ": the righteousness we gain in justification is not part of our being but is something that is and remains external to us. Charles Wesley's famous lines express this idea well:

No condemnation now I dread:
Jesus, and all in Him, is mine!
Alive in him, my living head,
And clothed in righteousness divine.

Luther's understanding of "righteousness" as external to us led him to criticize Augustine, who understood the righteousness in question to be part of our being. Luther and Augustine agreed that the righteousness through which we are justified is given to us by God and not something which we ourselves can acquire—but they did not agree on the *nature* of that righteous-ness. For Augustine, justifying righteousness is an *internal* righteousness, something God works *within* us; for Luther, it is *external*, something God works *outside* us. And it is the development of this idea of an "external" or "alien righteous-ness" that led to the establishment of the characteristically Protestant idea of *forensic justification*. We shall consider this idea, as developed by Melanchthon and John Calvin.

Melanchthon gives the following definition of justification: "To be justified does not mean that an ungodly man is made righteous, but that he is *pronounced righteous in a forensic manner*." Augustine had interpreted the Latin verb *iustificare*("to justify") as *iustum facere* ("to make righteous"), but Melanchthon eliminates this idea: justification is about being *declared or pronounced righteous*, not being *made righteous*. Similarly, Calvin defines justification as "the remission of sins and the imputation of the righteousness of Christ." A distinc-tion is made between *justification* and *sanctification* (or *regenera-tion*): the former is the work of God outside us, the latter his work within us. In effect, Melanchthon and Calvin distinguish two aspects of the process that both Augustine and the young Luther had treated as a single unit. Thus Augustine taught that justification embraces all of Christian existence, including both the *event* of being treated as righteous and the *process* of becoming righteous. For Melanchthon and Calvin, however, the event (justification) and the process (sanctification) could be and should be distinguished. The forgiveness of sins and the renewing gift of the Holy Spirit are to be treated as logically distinct.

Why should this distinction have been introduced and what is its significance?[7] To understand this, we need to consider the doctrines of justification associated with Zwingli and Bucer, two early Reformed theologians who rose to prominence before John Calvin. It is often overlooked that early Reformed theology was strongly moralistic. Zwingli's chief concern was with reforming the morals, structures, and practices of the church of his day and bringing them in line with Scripture. Zwingli argued that Christian morality consists in following the example of Jesus Christ, and that justification took place as a result of this imitation of Christ (an idea already found in the writings of Erasmus of Rotterdam). *The moral regeneration of the individual was thus the cause of his justification.*

The early Reformed theologians therefore viewed Luther's teaching on justification with alarm, as it seemed to them (quite wrongly, as it happened) to break the link between morality and religion. Luther had insisted that the sinner is justified without any reference to his works, regeneration, or moral character. On the other hand, it seemed to the critics of Zwingli's teaching (rightly!) that it was simply works-righteousness: individuals were justified on the basis of their works (in this case "moral regeneration," which was obviously a human achievement). Furthermore, it seemed to the critics (again, rightly) that Christ was only involved in Zwingli's theology of justification in an external manner: Christ provides the moral example we are supposed to imitate, and when we do this, we are justified. But according to Luther, Christ comes to dwell within the believer and is involved with his existence internally. And so it became essential to clarify the Reformed teaching on justification to ensure that several elements were preserved:

1. The total gratuity of our reconciliation with God had to be upheld.
2. The necessity of regeneration and good works had to be upheld.
3. Christ had to be involved *internally* in the process.

It was due to the genius of John Calvin that this difficulty was completely overcome—in fact, so successful was Calvin's solution that it was adopted by just about every Lutheran theologian as well, despite Luther's somewhat different views on the matter. Calvin argued like this. The gospel concerns our encounter with Jesus Christ and our union with him. What we receive from God is not a series of gifts, but one supreme gift— the gracious indwelling of Jesus Christ himself. In making this assertion, Calvin clearly develops the authentic New Testament insight that the believer is incorporated into the life of the risen Christ. Calvin thus integrates Christ into the life of faith in an *internal*, rather than a purely *external*, manner. To meet Christ in this way is to be born again as a new creation (2 Cor. 5:17).

This union with Christ has two main consequences. Calvin,

basing himself on 1 Corinthians 6:11, refers to them as the "double grace" of *justification* and *sanctification*. These two are given to us simultaneously as aspects of our union with Christ. They cannot be separated from that union, nor from one another. In other words, apart from union with Christ there can be no justification and no sanctification. And justification cannot exist without sanctification, since both are given together, simultaneously. The following extended quotation from Calvin makes this point perfectly:

> Christ "is made unto us wisdom and righteousness, and sanctification and redemption" (1 Cor. 1:30). Christ, therefore, justifies no man without also sanctifying him. Those blessings are joined by a perpetual and inseparable tie. Those whom he enlightens by his wisdom, he redeems; whom he redeems, he justifies; whom he justifies, he sanctifies. But as the question relates only to justification and sanctification, to them let us confine ourselves. Though we distinguish between them, they are both inseparably comprehended in Christ. Would you then obtain justification in Christ? You must previously possess Christ. But you cannot possess him without being made a partaker of his sanctification: for Christ cannot be divided. Since the Lord, therefore, does not grant us the enjoyment of these blessings without bestowing himself, he bestows both at once, but never the one without the other. Thus it appears how true it is that we are justified not *without*, and yet not *by* works, since in the participation of Christ, by which we are justified, is contained not less sanctification than justification.[8]

In other words, although justification and sanctification may be *distinguished*, they cannot be *separated*. In that our redemptive encounter and union with Christ are totally free and unmerited, the gratuity of justification is upheld—just as the unbreakable link between the union with Christ and sanctification upholds the necessity of both regeneration and sanctification. Justification is still treated as the external pronouncement of God that we are right in his sight—but the pronouncement is made on the basis of the presence within us of the living Christ.

This distinction between justification and sanctification has led to considerable confusion. What the first fifteen hundred years of the Christian church had called "justification" now had to be split into two parts, one of which was still called "justification"! In practice, the reader may use the term "justification" *either* to mean the creative and redemptive encounter of the individual with the risen Christ (the sense used by Augustine, the young Luther, and in the systematic sections of the present work) *or* in the sense of the declaration that the believer is in the right, linked to (but distinct from!) sanctification and regeneration. The important point is that the reader must be clear which understanding is being used, especially when discussing such matters with anyone else. It may be that differences of opinion arise because different definitions of the same term are used!

A further point of importance concerns the grounds of assurance and is best seen by comparing Zwingli and Calvin. For Zwingli, the individual is justified on account of his moral regeneration. In effect, God endorses his moral regeneration. The grounds of assurance are thus located in the individual, who is under obligation to ensure that he is sufficiently regenerated to merit his justification (the use of the word "merit," by the way, is deliberate—Zwingli teaches a doctrine of justification by works). For Calvin, however, the key right-making maneuver takes place outside the believer by an act of God's grace. The believer may therefore rest assured—in a manner not permitted by Zwingli—that all that needs to be done to initiate the Christian life has been done by God, allowing the believer to concentrate upon *living* his Christian life.

The concept of the "imputation of the righteousness of Christ," mentioned above, needs further discussion. For the later Reformers, such as Melanchthon and Calvin, the basis of our justification is the righteousness of Christ, earned through his obedience to God in his life and death. This righteousness, however, is always alien and external to us: we do not possess in ourselves sufficient righteousness upon which the verdict of divine justification may be based. The righteousness of Christ is thus "imputed" to us—in other words, it is treated as if it were ours, or reckoned to us, without ever *becoming* ours. Shielded by this aura of divine righteousness, the process of sanctification (in which we are gradually made righteous) may begin and develop. The Reformation doctrine of assurance, already noted above, is linked with this understanding of both justification and justifying faith: Because it is God who supplies both the righteousness on the basis of which we are justified and the faith through which it is imputed to us, we may rest assured that all that needs to be done for our justification has been done—and has been done well.

A helpful way of distinguishing the Reformed understanding of the nature of justifying righteousness from that of Augustine or the Council of Trent is by using the concepts of *analytic* and *synthetic* divine judgment. For Augustine, the righteousness on the basis of which we are to be justified is already present within us, through the gracious action of God—and God therefore *analyzes* what is already there in order to justify us. But for Melanchthon and Calvin, there is no righteousness within us which could function as the basis of the divine verdict of justification—and God must therefore *synthesize* this righteousness himself.

An important factor in this sixteenth-century discussion was the new awareness of the forensic background of the Old Testament concept of justification, an awareness that resulted from new insights into the Hebrew language. Augustine and the medieval theologians had to rely upon Latin translations of the Old Testament texts, whereas the Reformers of the sixteenth century had direct access to the original Hebrew. It was largely for this reason that the distinction between "justification" (being *declared* righteous) and "sanctification" (being *made* righteous) was made. Of course, the Reformers were not suggesting that these two were separable, so that it was possible to be declared righteous without being made righteous! What they were doing was to draw attention to the misleading interpretation given to the term "justification" by Augustine and to try to correct him on this point. However, the Roman Catholic opponents of the Reformation misunderstood the Reformers to be suggesting that it was not necessary for a justified sinner to be regenerated, and they criticized the doctrine of forensic justification as a result.

The fierce controversy surrounding the views of Andreas Osiander—who argued for a doctrine of justification by inherent righteousness—served to consolidate Protestant opinion on the nature of justification and justifying righteousness, with the result that the following four characteristics of the Protestant doctrines of justification were established by the year 1540.

1. Justification is the forensic *declaration* that the Christian is righteous, rather than the process by which he or she is *made* righteous. It involves a change in *status* rather than in *nature*.
2. A deliberate and systematic distinction is made between justification (the external act by which God declares the believer to be righteous) and sanctification or regeneration (the internal process of renewal by the Holy Spirit).
3. Justifying righteousness is the alien righteousness of Christ, imputed to the believer and external to him, not a righteousness that is inherent within him, located within him, or in any way belonging to him.
4. Justification takes place *per fidem propter Christum*, with faith being understood as the God-given means of justification and the merits of Christ the God-given foundation of justification.

FOR FURTHER READING

For the development of the doctrine of justification at the time of the Reformation, see:

Alister E. McGrath. *Iustitia Dei: A History of the Christian Doctrine of Justification*. 2 vols. Cambridge: Cambridge University Press, 1986. 2:1–53.

For more general reading:

Paul Althaus. *The Theology of Martin Luther*. Philadelphia: Fortress, 1966.

Roland H. Bainton. *Here I Stand: A Life of Martin Luther*. New York: Scribner, 1950.

Wilhelm Dantine. *The Justification of the Ungodly*. St. Louis: Concordia, 1968.

Gerhard O. Forde. *Justification by Faith—A Matter of Death and Life.* Philadelphia: Fortress, 1982.

Alister E. McGrath. *Luther's Theology of the Cross: Martin Luther's Theological Breakthrough.* New York: Basil Blackwell, 1985.

_____. *The Intellectual Origins of the European Reformation.* New York: Basil Blackwell, 1987. 32–122.

_____. *Reformation Thought: An Introduction.* New York: Basil Blackwell, 1988. 67–94.

Jaroslav Pelikan. *The Christian Tradition: A History of the Development of Doctrine: 4. Reformation of Church and Dogma (1300–1700).* Chicago and London: University of Chicago Press, 1984. 127–82.

5 DENOMINATIONAL DIFFERENCES

Since the European Reformation of the sixteenth century, a significant number of Christian denominations have developed. In this chapter we will survey the opinions of the main Christian denominations on the doctrine of justification by faith. This survey is not intended to be exhaustive but merely to sketch and compare highlights.

First, it should be noted that it is the Western churches who have chosen to pay most attention to the doctrine of *justification*. The Eastern churches—such as the Greek and Russian Orthodox churches—have always preferred to discuss the redemption of humanity in terms of the image of *deification*.[1]

A second point that should be noted is the general agreement among most Protestant denominations concerning the doctrine of justification. Although there are indeed differences between the Lutheran and Reformed positions,[2] these differences either are somewhat technical or else are tied in with the related doctrines of predestination and election. Similarly, there are some areas of divergence between Lutheran and Reformed theology on the one hand and Pietist versions of these on the other; again, these disagreements tend to be somewhat technical.[3] The most important historical disagreement on justification has, of course, been between the Protestant churches on the one hand and the Roman Catholic church on the other. Yet even between these there exists a large measure of agreement, as will be shown at the end of this chapter.

With this in mind, we now proceed to a point-by-point comparison of the views of Protestant denominations and Roman Catholicism on a number of points on which disagreement exists. These are:

1. What is understood by "justification"?
2. What is understood by "justification by faith"?
3. What is the nature of justifying righteousness?
4. May an individual be said to merit justification?

We shall consider these questions individually, basing our analysis on the historical confessional documents of the respective denominations. It is, of course, necessary to note that some modern Protestants do not feel themselves bound by these documents (for example, modern Anglicans tend to pay little attention to the Thirty-Nine Articles). This analysis will, however, clarify the respective *historical* positions adopted by the various denominations on the matters in question. With this point in mind, we may turn to the first question.

1. What Is Understood by "Justification"?

The Council of Trent defined the Roman Catholic understanding of justification as follows: "The movement from the state in which man is born a son of the first Adam to the state of grace and adoption as sons of God through the second Adam, our savior Jesus Christ." Justification is thus understood as involving the entire transition from nature to grace, involving both the event by which the Christian life is begun and the process by which it is developed and finally consummated. In many ways, this understanding of justification parallels that of Augustine of Hippo.

The Protestant denominations have defined justification primarily in forensic terms, as the act of God by which the sinner is declared to be righteous. The *event* of justification (by which God declares the individual to be righteous) is to be distinguished from the *process* of sanctification (in which the individual is regenerated and renewed through the action of the Holy Spirit). Justification is thus an act of God external to the sinner, and sanctification is the action of God within him. Although justification and sanctification can be distinguished in theory, in practice they are inseparable: whoever is justified is also sanctified. In the previous chapter (p. 58), we noted

Calvin's emphatic statements on this matter. The words of John Wesley are also helpful here, despite the old-fashioned English:

> Though it be allowed that justification and the new birth are, in point of time, inseparable from each other, yet they are easily distinguished, as not being the same, but things of a widely different nature. Justification implies only a relative, the new birth a real, change. God in justifying does something *for* us; in begetting us again, he does the work *in* us. The former changes our outward relation to God, so that of enemies we become children; by the latter, our inmost souls are changed, so that of sinners we become saints.[4]

It will therefore be obvious that the Roman Catholic understands by "justification" what the Protestant understands by "justification" *and* "sanctification" linked together. The same word is used by both—but it has a different meaning in each case. This has led to enormous confusion. Consider the following two statements.

A. We are justified by faith alone.
B. We are justified by faith and works.

The former broadly corresponds to the Protestant, the latter to the Roman Catholic position. But what do they mean?

For the Protestant, statement A means that the Christian life is begun through faith, and faith alone, which appears to be the New Testament teaching on the question. For the Roman Catholic, however—who understands "justification" in a different way—statement A means that the Christian life *as a whole* is begun and continued by faith alone, which seems to exclude any reference to regeneration or obedience. For the Roman Catholic, statement B means that the Christian life is begun in faith, but is continued and developed through obedience and good works—which appears to be the general position of the New Testament. But the Protestant—who understands "justification" to refer only to the *beginning* of the Christian life—would regard this as a totally unacceptable doctrine of justification by works. In fact, there is general agreement between Protestant and Roman Catholic that the

Christian life is *begun* through faith and *continued and developed* through obedience and good works—the Reformation slogan "faith is pregnant with good works" embodies this principle.

Protestants are often accused by their opponents of developing a totally fictitious concept of justification—of suggesting that the believer lives in a sort of Walter Mitty world in which he is treated as righteous when he is actually nothing of the sort. The phrase "legal fiction" is often used to describe or discredit this concept of justification. But the forensic understanding of justification merely highlights the fact that sinners have nothing to contribute to their own justification—an insight shared with even those who do *not* adopt a forensic understanding of justification! There is nothing within the sinner that can ever be said to constitute the basis or grounds of his justification—those must be provided by none other than God himself. Justification does not depend upon, or follow, transformation and regeneration—only if justification is understood to follow, or to be based on, transformation or regeneration is there any substance to this criticism. In fact, the view that justification is based on and contingent on moral regeneration is associated with the Enlightenment and represents an abandonment of the idea of justification by grace in favor of justification by merit. The Protestant understanding of the nature of both justification and justifying righteousness is simply one way of emphasizing that it is God who both establishes the grounds for our justification and provides the means by which that justification may be appropriated, which is in agreement with the strongly forensic overtones of the Hebrew verb "to justify."

2. What Is Meant by "Justification by Faith"?

The basic point is that it is *God* who justifies us. The slogan *sola fide*("by faith alone") emphasizes the total incapacity of humanity for any kind of self-justification. The grounds of our justification lie in the gracious promises of God, and not in any moral actions or works of any kind which we may perform. *All* our salvation comes to us by faith. This faith is not a blind, dogmatic obedience or an arrogant boasting, but is a firm and humble trust in which we look to God as the gracious and faithful author of our salvation and believe in his promises of mercy—recognizing that even our faith, through which we come to trust in God, is nothing other than a gracious gift given to us, rather than something which we ourselves accomplish. In recent years, there has been a growing awareness that Roman Catholics and Protestants have several important insights into this doctrine in common. Thus the Council of Trent insisted upon the priority of faith over everything else in justification. "Faith is the beginning of human salvation, the foundation and root of all justification, without which it is impossible to please God." Similarly, the Reformers insisted upon faith as the sole instrument of justification. In justification, we receive by faith the effects of the work of Christ on our behalf, appropriating it and making it our own. Justifying faith is not just historical knowledge (which the English Reformer William Tyndale called a "story-book faith") or intellectual conviction, but a trustful, self-involving response to the gospel. We are justified *per fidem propter Christum* (through faith on account of Christ): The objective basis of our justification is the person and work of Jesus Christ, and the means by which we appropriate this justification and make it our own is faith. To repeat: justification by faith does *not* mean that we are justified *on account* of our faith, but that we are justified on account of *Christ* through the grace of God. Faith must always be acknowledged as the work of God within us.

3. What Is the Nature of Justifying Righteousness?

Just as a major historical difference exists between Protestants and Roman Catholics concerning the nature of justification, so a corresponding difference exists with regard to the question of justifying righteousness. For the Protestant, justifying righteousness is the alien righteousness of Christ which is imputed to the believer. It never becomes part of the believer or can be said to belong to him; it is "reckoned" or "imputed" to him. The believer remains a sinner, but he is counted as righteous in the sight of God: he is *simul iustus et peccator* (righteous and a sinner at one and the same time). Indeed, it is God's justification of the sinner that fully demonstrates the extent of his sinfulness. The Heidelberg Catechism states this as follows:

Q. How are you righteous before God?
A. Only by true faith in Jesus Christ. In spite of the fact that my conscience accuses me that I have grievously sinned against all the commandments of God, and that I have failed to keep any of them, and that I am still ever prone to all that is evil, yet God, without any merit of my own, out of pure grace, grants me the benefits of the perfect expiation of Christ, imputing to me his righteousness and holiness, as if I had never committed a single sin or had ever been sinful, having fulfilled myself all the obedience which Christ has carried out for me, if only I accept such favor with a trusting heart.[5]

For the Roman Catholic, however, justifying righteousness is inherent in the believer, part of his person. Although it is a gift of God bestowed upon the sinner, it may be said to be part of the sinner's being. The sanctifying action of the Holy Spirit removes the guilt of sin and renders the believer righteous in the sight of God. To use a distinction introduced earlier (p. 60), Protestants understand justification to be based on a *synthetic* divine judgment, whereas Roman Catholics understand it to be based on an *analytic* divine judgment.[6]

Protestants tend to be suspicious of the concept of an inherent justifying righteousness, which they fear may cause the believer to become either complacent or anxious and thus to fail to rely completely upon the mercy and grace of God. In addition, the possibility that this "inherent righteousness" might be confused with a *human* righteousness gained by good works has caused serious anxieties in Protestant circles in that this misunderstanding immediately opens the way for a doctrine of justification by works. Roman Catholics, on the other hand, tend to be suspicious of the concept of an external or alien justifying righteousness, fearing that the idea could lead to the neglect of good works and Christian obedience. It is clear that these anxieties may be based on misunderstanding. It is important to realize that Roman Catholics as well as Protestants teach that the righteousness of the individual, upon which his justification is based, is itself provided by God. For both, justification remains an act of God based upon an objective foundation provided and established by God himself. The Protestant understanding of the nature of justifying righteousness has the advantage of bringing out the forensic and declaratory overtones of the Old Testament idea of "justifying," while emphasizing that the righteousness in question is not a human righteousness, acquired through the performance of good works—but properly understood, this is not what the Roman Catholic view implies.

4. May an Individual Be Said to Merit Justification?

There is general agreement between Roman Catholics and Protestants that justification is a totally free and unmerited act of God that is not the result of our works or achievements. Justification will always remain an act of divine graciousness. To suggest that an individual can earn his justification is Pelagian and quite incompatible with the Christian gospel. The suggestion that an individual can merit his justification is actually associated with the rationalistic Enlightenment, rather than with Roman Catholicism.

Yet the Roman Catholic teaching on merit is open to a number of misunderstandings, in part because of the slightly confusing terms used by Roman Catholic theologians to discuss it. Some Roman Catholic theologians make a distinction between two types of merit: merit in the strict sense of the word, meaning something God is under obligation to reward ("condign" merit), and merit in a weak sense of the word, meaning something to which it is appropriate that God should respond ("congruous" merit).[7] All Roman Catholic theologians insist that it is impossible that an individual should *in the strict sense of the word* merit justification, although some allow that justification may be "merited" *in the weak sense of the term*. The idea of "congruous" merit has been viewed with intense suspicion by Protestants, who tend to regard it as having Pelagian overtones.

The Council of Trent taught that individuals gain merit in the strict sense of the term *after justification*. Although this doctrine is understood to be an attempt to express the New Testament's views on the rewards given to believers as a result of their good works, this doctrine has been criticized by Protestants as tending to undermine trust in God alone for salvation. Even though the Council of Trent emphasized that these rewards are the consequence of divine generosity rather than human endeavor, its critics pointed out that it tends in practice to lead to the individual believer coming to trust in his own efforts as the basis of salvation. The real problem here, however, lies in the use of the term "merit" in the first place.

In an earlier chapter (p. 35), we pointed out how Tertullian was responsible for introducing the rather unhelpful translation *liberum arbitrium* into the theological vocabulary of the Western church. It may not come as much of a surprise, therefore, to learn that it was this same person who introduced the Latin term *meritum* as a translation for the Greek word for "reward." *Meritum* came from the field of Roman law (Tertullian, remember, was a lawyer) and had legal overtones that came to pass into theology. Once more, it was Augustine who managed to rescue the Western church from a serious misunderstanding of the idea. While the word "merit" had become so well established that it was virtually impossible to stop using it, Augustine managed to recover a more authentic biblical insight. For Augustine, "merit" is not something we may claim because of what we have achieved, but *something God gives to us on account of who he is*. The initiative is always understood, by Augustine and by the New Testament, as coming from God (who *gives*), rather than from human individuals (who *claim*).

Protestants and Roman Catholics, therefore, are united in asserting that we have no claim whatsoever upon God for our justification: it is something *God gives us*, something *God does for us*. However, it must be noted that a difference develops concerning the role of merit in the Christian life itself. While Protestants are content to speak of God rewarding our efforts as believers, Roman Catholics speak of believers gaining merit. The Catholic approach is regarded with some suspicion by Protestants, in that it appears to place an unhealthy emphasis upon achievements and the claim they allow us to make upon God, instead of emphasizing the divine generosity towards us.

On the basis of the above analysis, it will be clear that there exist real differences between Protestants and Roman Catholics over the matter of justification. The question remains, however, as to the significance of these differences. How important, for example, is the distinction between an alien and an intrinsic justifying righteousness? In recent years, there appears to be increasing sympathy for the view that these differences, although of importance in the Reformation period, no longer possess the significance that they once had. This is not to say that the Christian denominations are agreed on the matter of justification, for it is obvious that their respective teachings have a very different "feel" or "atmosphere" to them. It seems that in the modern period the Christian denominations have preferred to concentrate on their points of agreement, rather than draw attention to their historical disagreements!

This may be due in part to an increasing recognition that today the real threat to the gospel of grace comes from the rationalism of the Enlightenment rather than from other Christian denominations. The Enlightenment promoted the idea that God can only justify morally renewed individuals; the idea that God justifies *sinners*, just as they are here and now, was rejected as contrary to both reason and morality. In many ways, the Enlightenment marked the rebirth of Pelagianism, with a new emphasis upon human moral capabilities and responsibilities.[8] Before an individual may be accepted by God, he must first make himself acceptable by becoming a good person. And so the Enlightenment, like the Pelagianism of the fifth century, developed a doctrine of the "justification of the *godly*," which was totally opposed to the gospel concept of the "justification of the *ungodly*."

The following points of agreement among the Christian denominations, including both the Protestant and Roman Catholic churches, are now widely recognized.

1. As a result of original sin, all human beings—whoever they are and whenever and wherever they live—stand in need of justification.

2. Christians have no hope of final salvation and no basis for justification before God other than through God's free gift of grace in Christ, offered to them through the Holy Spirit. Our

entire hope of justification and salvation rests on the promises of God and the saving work of Jesus Christ, expressed in the gospel.

3. Justification is a completely free act of God's grace, and nothing we can do can be said to be the basis or ground of our own justification. Even faith itself must be recognized as a divine gift and work within us. We cannot turn to God unless God turns us first. The priority of God's redeeming will and action over our own actions in bringing about our salvation is expressed by the doctrine of predestination.

4. In justification we are declared righteous before God, and the process of making us righteous in his sight through the renewing action of the Holy Spirit is begun. In that justification, we receive by faith the effects of the death and resurrection of Jesus Christ as we respond personally to the gospel, the power of God for salvation, as we encounter the gospel through scripture, the proclamation of the word of God, and the sacraments, and as it initially awakens and subsequently strengthens faith in us.

5. Whoever is justified is subsequently renewed by the Holy Spirit and motivated and enabled to perform good works. This is not to say that individuals may rely upon these works for their salvation, because eternal life remains a gift offered to us through the grace and mercy of God.

FOR FURTHER READING

For a general survey of the doctrines of justification associated with Lutheran, Reformed, and Anglican churches, the Council of Trent, and also Puritans and Pietists, see:

Alister E. McGrath. *Iustitia Dei: A History of the Christian Doctrine of Justification*. 2 vols. Cambridge: Cambridge University Press, 1986. 2:1–53, 63–86, 98–134.

For a point-by-point comparison of Lutheran, Reformed, and Roman Catholic views, see:

Wilhelm Niesel. *The Gospel and the Churches*. Philadelphia: Westminster, 1962.

For a classic comparison of the views of the Council of Trent and Karl Barth, see:

Hans Küng. *Justification: The Doctrine of Karl Barth and a Catholic Reflection.* 2nd ed. Philadelphia: Westminster, 1981.

For criticism of this book, see:

Alister E. McGrath. "Justification: Barth, Trent and Küng." *Scottish Journal of Theology* 34 (1981): 517–29.

For two recent documents recording at least a degree of agreement between Protestants and Roman Catholics, see:

"Justification by Faith" [Report of the Lutheran-Roman Catholic Dialogue Group in the United States], *Origins* 13/17(1983):277–304.

Salvation and the Church: An Agreed Statement by the Second Anglican-Roman Catholic International Commission, London: Church House Publishing/Catholic Truth Society, 1987.

Part Two

The Contemporary Significance of the Doctrine

6   THE EXISTENTIAL DIMENSION

Modern Western humanity tends to judge its spiritual state in terms of categories such as "meaning," "fulfillment," and "purpose." Where the theologians of the sixteenth-century Reformation or the eighteenth-century Great Awakening directed their preaching towards "law" and "guilt," the modern preacher must learn to direct his proclamation of the gospel to the felt needs of modern humanity. He must become receptor-oriented, sensitive to the needs, fears, and aspirations of his audience, in order to gain a point of contact, a toehold by which his proclamation may be grounded in the existential situation of hearers. What he has to proclaim must be seen to relate to modern human existence.

As we emphasized earlier (p. 12), this does not mean compromising or distorting the gospel proclamation to suit the preoccupations of modern Western humanity—rather, it means taking the trouble to determine how the gospel, with its richness and multifaceted character, impinges upon modern humanity. *The transformation of human existence depends upon prior correlation with that existence.* It is the task of the theologian to aid and support the work of the preacher by becoming the translator and interpreter of the gospel of justification by faith into contemporary Western categories. It is necessary for the theologian to wrestle with the religious, cultural, social, and political realities of his own situation, *in order to be relevant to that situation*—just as he must also wrestle with the scriptural witness and history of scriptural interpretation *if he is to be faithful to the gospel.* The theologian must engage in a dialectical and dialogical approach, moving back and forth from the gospel center of free justification in Jesus Christ to the context and situation to which it is to be proclaimed. The gospel both addresses and challenges the presuppositions of that context— but before the process of criticism may begin, it is necessary that a real engagement between gospel and context takes place and a real connection between the two is established.[1]

Contemporary existentialist philosophies offer the modern Western theologian a point of contact with the existential concerns of modern Western humanity and a possible means of bridging the gap between the Christian proclamation of justification by faith and modern ways of thinking about ultimate concerns. In this chapter, we propose to illustrate how this may be done by considering the structures of human existence as uncovered by contemporary existentialist analysis. We begin by briefly outlining some aspects of existentialist thought.

1. The Basics of Existentialism

Who are we? Why are we here? Why do we exist? What does it *mean* to exist? All of us exist in the world—yet we are often aware of an uncomfortable sense of not being quite at home there, of being anxious about our existence, of feeling threatened and worried by the inevitability of death. We feel that our existence is threatened by forces over which we have little or no control—forces such as social pressures and political manipulation on the one hand, and mortality, death, and finitude on the other.

A human being, a stone, and a tree all *exist* in that they are all unquestionably part of the same world. And yet, ever since human beings began to think, they have been aware of some fundamental, though perhaps undefinable, distinction between themselves on the one hand and all other forms of life on the other. But what *is* this difference? The entire career of human philosophy has concerned itself with trying to cast light on this crucial question.

Perhaps the most important thing that distinguishes human beings from other forms of life is the fact that human beings are aware of their own existence and ask questions about it. The rise of existentialist philosophy is ultimately a response to this crucial insight.[2] We not only exist—we *are aware* and we *understand* that we exist, and we are aware that our existence will one day be terminated by death. The sheer fact of our existence is important to us and we find it difficult, probably impossible, to adopt a totally detached attitude towards it. Existentialist philosophy is basically a protest against the view that human beings are "things" and a demand that we take the personal existence of the individual with full seriousness. Each of us is an individual and defies general classification. We cannot be defined just in terms of our social security number— we are individuals, and our individuality is important to us.

This distinction between ourselves and objects or things is brought out with special clarity by the highly influential German existentialist philosopher Martin Heidegger in his analysis of the structures of human existence. Heidegger draws a distinction between the mode of existence of a human being, aware of his own existence (*Dasein*), and the mode of existence of an inanimate object, a thing (*Vorhandenheit*—literally, "being at hand"). And Heidegger emphasizes that there is every danger that *Dasein* will become *Vorhandenheit*—in other words, that our existence will be reduced to the level of things. We can get so tied up and concerned with things, with the world, that we lose our distinctive identities as individuals. We become a member of a crowd, as our individual identity is swallowed up and lost.

This point is also expressed in terms of the difference between "objective" and "subjective" knowledge. "Objective" knowledge involves knowing about something in a theoretical or detached manner, rather like a scientist examining samples of blood or a statistician analyzing consumer trends. Although these impersonal figures and statistics are ultimately based on individuals, those individuals are lost in a mass of impersonal data. Individuals just don't matter here. More importantly, the scientist or statistician must *eliminate* his own personal feelings from his work, so that he can adopt a totally neutral and detached approach to the subject. There is no doubt that this is important—but, as we shall emphasize later (p. 149), there is no real possibility of a neutral, disinterested, or objective knowledge *of God*, simply because we realize that we ourselves, our own personal existence, is bound up with his existence. Subjective knowledge involves knowing something which is of importance to our own personal existence. The distinction between "objective" and "subjective" knowledge is probably best brought out in relation to the knowledge of death.

Death may be treated objectively as a biological phenomenon, as the termination of the life-process. The physiological changes in humans associated with the phenomenon may be objectively described and recorded. But this is dealing with *somebody else's death*. To treat death as an existential phenomenon, however, is to recognize that the future event of *our own death* already enters into our way of thinking and exercises influence over us. To be born is already to be on the way to death. There is no way we can avoid it. And every now and then something happens to remind us of the fact that we must die—perhaps a relative or close friend dies, and we are forced to reflect on the fact that we too must die. This is subjective knowledge—the awareness of something that affects our individual existence (in this case, by bringing home to us that it won't go on forever!) This recognition of the inevitability of death, of the fact that existence as we know it will one day be terminated, causes us anxiety (the German word *Angst* is often used to refer to this "existential anxiety").

It is for this reason that contemporary existential philosophy has placed great emphasis upon "subjective" knowledge—an approach exemplified by the Danish philosopher Kierkegaard in his famous affirmation "truth is subjectivity." By "subjective" he did not mean "prejudiced," "unreliable," or "biased," as the usual sense of the word would imply. Rather, he meant that the personal concerns of the individual cannot be ignored in the search for truth. "Truth" is not just about intellectual theories or concepts, involving just the human mind, but it is about the whole person, the whole of human existence. Our emotions and our wills, our passions as well as our intellects, must be caught up and involved in our search for truth. Truth must be personally relevant if it is to transform us and our existence. For this reason, existentialism—while not having any quarrel with objective scientific truth!—has emphasized the need for the subjective relevance of truth if it is to affect the way we are, the way we exist. If we are to encounter the "truth that sets us free," that truth must be something that grasps us and changes us inwardly, rather than something we just know

with our minds. Head knowledge must become heart knowledge. A distinction often made by existentialist thinkers is
between *knowing about the truth* (in other words, objective truth)
and *being grasped by the truth* (in other words, subjective truth).
And it is with this latter that the doctrine of justification is
concerned—*subjective knowledge of God as redeemer through Jesus
Christ.*

2. *The Existential Analysis of Human Existence*

Existentialism draws a careful distinction between two modes
of existence, two ways of existing in the world, that are open to
individuals. Following Heidegger, these ways of existing are
usually referred to as "authentic existence" and "inauthentic
existence." An individual who exists authentically may be said
to be existing in such a way as to fulfill his potential as a human
being. In this state, he may be said to have fulfillment, purpose,
and meaning. In inauthentic existence, on the other hand, an
individual loses his distinctive capacities and identity. He is
trapped by forces he cannot master and is a slave to illusions
about the nature of existence. He refuses to face up to the
realities of life, such as death and finitude. His whole life is a
sham, and he probably knows it.

Unlike animals, human beings know at the cognitive or
intellectual level that they must die, but they are reluctant to
accept this fact existentially. In other words, they know that
one day they will die (and may even joke about it!), but find it
difficult—and even distressing—to reflect seriously on the fact
that one day they, as individual human beings, will cease to
exist. Individuals cannot bear the thought of death. It is
threatening to think of the world going on without them. The
thought of finitude is deeply distressing to many individuals,
who tend to make the denial of this eventuality their life
projects. The seductiveness of the words of the serpent to Eve
lie in the fact that they suggest that death is *not* inevitable: "You
will not surely die . . . you will be like God" (Gen. 3:4–5). And
so humanity becomes trapped within its own lie, as it tries to
deny death and protect itself against it. Fallen humanity is
tempted to base its entire existence upon a delusion and a lie,

and feels threatened by the possibility of the exposure of this lie. And yet the way to authentic existence is through facing the realities of human existence—such as our death and finitude.

Heidegger speaks of individuals "falling" away from a state of authentic existence, or being "alienated" from authentic existence. For Heidegger, this "fallenness" or "alienation" can come about through obsession with transitory things or through becoming absorbed into a crowd and losing individual identity. Conversely, this fallenness and alienation may be overcome by adopting a correct attitude towards existence. And the first step in this process, according to Heidegger, is the *disclosure of inauthenticity*. In other words, something happens to make you aware that you're living a lie, that you are running away from the realities of existence. Existential anxiety (*Angst*) is perhaps the most important of these realities, and this is often grounded in the fear of death.

The anticipation of death brings home to us the fact that our existence is transitory, and that we are living in a state of delusion, of inauthentic existence, if we base our existence upon this world and its goods. Fallen humanity is tempted to overlook death, despite its importance, precisely because it *wants* to overlook it. Heidegger thus emphasizes that existential anxiety in the face of death discloses to individuals that they are living a lie if they cannot cope with it, that their whole existence is based upon a delusion unless they face up to its reality and inevitability and re-orient themselves accordingly. And because *Angst* is so threatening, much of Western society prefers to ignore death or marginalize it, if it cannot be denied completely.

This brief analysis of the two categories of human existence—authentic and inauthentic—allows us to take the next step in our discussion. We may now ask how the gospel links up with these categories and how it may be articulated and explained in their terms.

3. Existence and the Gospel

The New Testament recognizes two quite distinct modes of human existence: an unbelieving, unredeemed form of existence, based on illusions and lies, and a believing and redeemed existence, in which the human existential potential is brought to its fullness. Similarly, the New Testament recognizes the need to disclose to humanity that its unbelieving and unredeemed mode of existence is inauthentic, in order that the way may be opened to authentic existence—life in all its redeemed fullness.

These two modes of human existence are both developed at great length in Scripture. For example, it is clear that a major element in the story of the Fall (Gen. 3) concerns the desire on the part of humanity to dispense with God in order to become self-sufficient. Here, the individual refuses to recognize himself for what he really is—a creature of God, dependent on him for his well-being and salvation. The individual seeks to justify himself by trying to secure his existence through moral actions or material prosperity. He tries to gain his essential nature, his authentic way of existence, through his own powers. His entire way of life is bound up with what is transitory, and so his life is subject to transitoriness and death. This individual lives in dependence upon the world, upon things that must ultimately pass away. And it is this attempt at self-sufficiency on the part of humanity that both the Old and New Testaments designate as "sin."

Over against this inauthentic mode of human existence the New Testament sets the mode of believing, redeemed existence, in which we abandon all security created by ourselves and place our trust in God. We recognize the illusion of our self-sufficiency and trust instead in the sufficiency of God. Instead of denying that we are God's creatures, we recognize and exult in this fact and base our existence upon it. Instead of clinging to transitory things for security, we learn to abandon faith in this transitory world in order that we may place our trust in something eternal—God himself. Instead of trying to justify ourselves, we learn to recognize that God offers us our justification as a free gift. Instead of denying the reality of our human finitude and the inevitability of death, we recognize that these have been faced and conquered through the death and resurrection of Jesus Christ, whose victory becomes our victory through faith. Christ shared in our humanity "so that by his death he might destroy him who holds the power of death—

that is, the devil—and free those who all their lives were held in slavery by their fear of death" (Heb. 2:14–15).

It is God who has the "knowledge of good and evil" (Gen. 2:16–17), and by attempting to gain this knowledge for itself, humanity demonstrates its perennial tendency to seek after self-sufficiency—to "be like God, knowing good and evil" (Gen. 3:5). Similarly, the Pelagian heresy (see pp. 33–44) is perhaps the most natural of all heresies in that it involves the suggestion that we are the masters of our own destiny. Humanity has always been tempted to believe in the seductive suggestion that it possesses the resources necessary for salvation and need not rely upon God for assistance. The temptation to boast in ourselves is continually countered by Paul, who points out that the only grounds for boasting we possess are Jesus Christ and his cross (1 Cor. 1:31; 2 Cor. 10:17; Gal. 6:14). Authentic human existence is only achieved through abandoning faith in ourselves and the world as the basis of our salvation, and by grounding our faith in God instead.

Similarly, the New Testament emphasizes the illusion of security created by material goods and human moral actions, in order to emphasize instead the promises of God as the only adequate basis for our security. Two famous affirmations from the Sermon on the Mount make this point with brilliance:

> Do not store up for yourselves treasures on earth, where moth and rust destroy, and where thieves break in and steal. But store up for yourselves treasures in heaven, where moth and rust do not destroy, and where thieves do not break in and steal. For where your treasure is, there your heart will be also (Matt. 6:19–21).

Two modes of existence are contrasted: the inauthentic mode of existence, based upon this world, which is transitory and temporary; and the authentic mode of existence, based on God himself, which involves rejection of any basis of trust in this world in order to place trust in God himself. The same point is made very forcefully by contrasting the man who built his house on the rock with the man who built his house on the sand (Matt. 7:24–27).

Both the New Testament and existentialism condemn the human tendency to conceal the ever-present possibility of death. Thus the parable of the rich fool (Luke 12:13–21) illustrates with some brilliance the human desire to flee from facing the reality of death and to rely on plans that exclude or overlook death. The perennial temptation is to justify ourselves by basing existence on human self-sufficiency or upon worldly goods—but death and decay show the temptation up for what it is: the allurement of an illusion. Instead, we are invited to base our existence upon God himself, the rock that nothing—not even death itself—can destroy or remove. The constantly repeated biblical emphasis upon God himself as the only basis for authentic human existence is accompanied by an equally persistent emphasis upon the inability of humanity to achieve authentic existence through its own efforts or through what the world has to offer.

At this point, we need to note one very important difference between the New Testament understanding of inauthentic existence and that associated with existentialist philosophers such as Heidegger. For Heidegger, inauthentic existence is *something we choose*. It is one of several options open to us. But for the New Testament, inauthentic existence is a *given*, not a choice. Whether we like it or not, we must all recognize that we enter the world already in a state of inauthentic existence, alienated from our true way of being.

The gospel reports the universal sinfulness of humanity. It is not primarily concerned with the question of *why* this should be the case: it simply declares that this *is* the case and that recognition of this fact is the starting point from which rectification of the situation can proceed. When a physician diagnoses an illness, his first concern is to establish what is wrong with his patient. His interest in how the condition arose is generally more academic. The same point may be made about the New Testament, which has relatively little interest in *how* we came to be sinners: the important thing is that God has addressed our condition directly in Jesus Christ. But there are some individuals—as there always have been, and probably always will be—who refuse to come to terms with the reality of universal human sinfulness unless it is explained and justified to them precisely how this situation arose. "*Why* are we sinful and alienated from our true mode of existence? Unless you explain to me why God allowed this situation to happen, I won't accept it or act upon it." The following point may prove useful in dealing with this objection.

There are a number of facts about human existence which we have to learn to accept, even if we don't understand why they are so in the first place. We may ask the question *why*, but a failure to give an answer to this question doesn't alter the situation. All of us must die. But why? Why were we created in such a way that we must die? Why can't we just go on living forever? But the fact that there aren't any especially convincing answers to these questions does not mean that we don't have to die! The fact that I can't explain why you're going to die won't keep you from dying! It doesn't *alter* the situation! It is simply a fact of life. Another fact of life is that humans reproduce sexually, and that this exercises an enormous influence over human behavior. But why should humans reproduce in this way? Why aren't we all hermaphrodites, able to reproduce without the need for a partner? Why don't we reproduce asexually, like an amoeba? And again, the answers given to these questions are not especially convincing. The simple answer is that this is the way things are, and no amount of refusing to accept that this is the way things are is going to alter the situation. The important thing which we all *do* in the end—is to accept that this is the way things are and to get on with life. And so it is with sin. It's just the way things are, and no amount of arguing about it is going to alter the situation. The important thing is how this situation may be altered, rather than quibbling about how it arose in the first place!

The Christian proclamation addresses our present existence and discloses (or confirms) its inauthenticity—and names it "sin." Just as we may come to know about the existence of God through contemplating the night sky and afterward have our views confirmed by Scripture and the Christian proclamation, so we may come to know about the inauthenticity of our existence through contemplating the inevitability of death and then have our views confirmed by Scripture and the Christian proclamation. Alternatively, just as we may come to realize through reading Scripture that God exists and then find our views confirmed by contemplating the night sky, so we may learn of the inauthenticity of our way of being through reading Scripture and then find our views confirmed through reflecting on the inevitability of death. In both cases, the same fundamental realization takes place. We realize that our natural mode of existence, which is tied up with the world and things that are temporal and transitory, is inauthentic, and we are moved to ask how our alienation from our true way of being may be abolished and overcome.

4. The Gospel and Authentic Existence

The New Testament proclaims that the universal human predicament of inauthentic existence can be transformed to a state of authentic existence. It is this insight that is encapsulated in the doctrine of justification by faith. The main elements of the New Testament proclamation of the possibility of authentic human existence are the following:

1. The recognition of the fallenness of humanity, of the alienation of humanity from its authentic existence.
2. The realization that we are offered authentic existence as a gift through the death and resurrection of Jesus Christ.
3. The embodiment of this authentic existence in the life of faith.

We shall consider each of these points individually.

The gospel affirms that humanity was created in the image of God (Gen. 1:26), with the intention that they would be the children of God. But by worshipping the creation instead of the creator, humanity has lost that possibility. We have become enslaved to the world—our being and concerns have become tied up with things that are transitory and material. We have become alienated from our true way of being, our authentic mode of existence. It will be clear that existentialism casts valuable light on the concept of original sin, which is understood as alienation from our true way of existence and being. The constant threat of death and extinction discloses to us the inauthenticity of this existence, and this *Angst* is the point of contact addressed by the Christian proclamation.

The doctrine of original sin is fundamentally an assertion that humanity is trapped in its existential situation and unable to extricate itself. If extrication from this situation is to take place, it must take place from outside the human situation. The idea of being trapped by forces we recognize as irrational but appear unable to break free from is only too familiar to us all. The streets of our cities bear depressing witness to the human tendency to be trapped by alcohol, drugs, gambling, and pornography, to name but the more obvious. We *know*, at the cognitive level, that it is absurd for a rational being to be trapped in this way—and yet we find it difficult to break free. Addiction provides a model of the more general human enslavement and bondage to sin.

Just as the individual who is hooked on cocaine may recognize that he is addicted, yet still remain unable to break free from the habit, so we may recognize that we are trapped within our human existential predicament—and yet that recognition does not bring liberation with it. For many theologians of the older liberal school, the recognition of one's predicament was virtually identical with liberation from it: by being enlightened with the truth it was possible to break free from delusions. You might think you were in a prison, but you were actually free—and once you realized this, you were able to live as a free individual. How shallow and naively optimistic an understanding of human nature underlies such a view! The streets of our cities bear witness to the grim realities of the human predicament, of human enslavement to forces lying beyond our control. The doctrine of justification proclaims that the human existential situation can be transformed through action from outside humanity, as God himself breaks into that situation and offers us authenticity as a gift. Although we ourselves are powerless to transform the fundamental cause of our predicament, God offers us precisely this transformation through the death and resurrection of Jesus Christ.

The gospel proclaims that fallen humanity is offered authentic existence *as a gift* through the death and resurrection of Jesus Christ. Authentic existence is not something that we can achieve, but is something that is offered to us by God himself. The gospel judges our present existence, condemns it as inauthentic in much the same way as a physician diagnoses an illness, and then offers us the possibility of abolishing our alienation from our true way of being. We are invited to abandon our attempts at self-sufficiency, to abandon our reliance upon things that are transitory, and instead to base our existence upon the promises of the eternal and living God.

For the New Testament, the achievement of our true nature is not something that *we* can attain, something that is at our disposal—that would be the way of self-justification, of justification by works. Every attempt on the part of fallen human individuals to justify themselves fails, since it is based upon the illusion of self-sufficiency. Human beings need to be liberated from their own situation by one who stands outside it. This liberation from the human situation thus takes place from outside humanity itself, in the life, death, and resurrection of Jesus Christ. It is God himself who intervenes in human history in order to make the attainment of authentic existence a genuine possibility for fallen humanity. We are set free to become ourselves, to become what we really are, through the grace of God, who does for us what we could never do for ourselves.

The word of justification is thus both the word of judgment and the word of life. It exposes and destroys our illusions about ourselves, revealing us as inadequate creatures of sin who must die. It also offers us the word of life in that it proclaims that death—the final event and boundary of finite human existence—has been confronted and overcome through the death and resurrection of Jesus Christ. The final event and boundary of believing and redeemed human existence is now the resurrection, not the event of death. Although the road to resurrection passes under the shadow of the cross, which cannot be avoided, we are reminded and reassured that Christ has trodden this road before us and promised eternal life to all who follow in his path. Death is not eliminated as an event in human existence—but it is shown to be the *penultimate* event, the gateway to resurrection, allowing human beings to transcend the bounds of their finite and mortal human existence through claiming by faith the power of the one who raised Christ Jesus from the dead. Inauthentic existence, characterized by the desire to deny sin, death, and mortality, gives way through faith to authentic existence, characterized by the willingness to confront the reality of death and claim Christ's victory over it as our own.

The New Testament proclaims this decisive alteration in the human situation in a number of images. The fallen and inauthentic mode of existence is designated as the way of darkness and death, and the way of authentic, believing, and redeemed existence as the way of light and life. It is helpful to remember that there are two Greek words that may be translated into English as "life." The Greek word *bios* corresponds to mere biological existence, the fact that we are alive and exist upon the face of the planet earth. The Greek word *zoe* is used by John's Gospel to mean "life in all its fullness," or "the full and authentic human existence" that transcends mere biological existence. Thus John declares that Jesus Christ has come into the world in order that we might have "life in all its fullness" (John 10:10; 20:31). It is Jesus Christ who brings life to the world. It is Jesus Christ who is the bread of life (John 6:35); it is he who is the resurrection and the life (John 11:25). Through the life, death, and resurrection of Jesus Christ, the authentic mode of existence which God intends for us becomes a present real possibility. That which we could never attain for ourselves is made available for us by God as a gift. The gospel promises eternal life to those who believe (John 6:40, 51, 53–58), and that eternal life manifests itself in the present as authentic, believing, and redeemed existence, a foretaste of what is yet to come.

A further point of interest may be made at this point. As is well known, John's Gospel emphasizes that God's judgment is not some totally future event but is inaugurated here and now. Judgment is *now*, in order that eternal life may begin *now* (John 12:31). The gospel proclamation passes judgment on our inauthentic existence, showing it up for what it really is. Just as the "light of the world" illuminates and thus exposes human sin (John 3:19–21), so Jesus Christ judges our mode of existence and condemns it as inauthentic—in order that we may act upon this judgment and seek authentic existence. But where is this authentic existence to be found? And how is it to be obtained? And then we realize that the same one who confronts us with the word of judgment is also the one who offers us the word of life. It is through the coming of Jesus Christ into the world and into our personal existence that sin is exposed for what it really is, and that our existence is transformed through his real and redeeming presence. It is through judgment (in other words, through exposure of our condition for what it really is) that we are saved. Jesus did not come merely to judge us, but to save us (John 12:44–47).

A similar point is made by Paul, particularly in his dialectic between "flesh" (*sarx*) and "spirit" (*pneuma*). Fallen inauthentic human existence is defined as existence "according to the flesh" (*kata sarka*), while authentic existence is defined as existence "according to the spirit" (*kata pneuma*).[3] The word "flesh" is not being used to refer to the human body or any specifically sexual aspects of human existence, but to a mode of human existence that is oriented away from God, towards the world and things that are tangible, temporary, and transitory. Similarly, the word "spirit" is not used to refer to some spiritual substance, but to a mode of human existence that is oriented towards faith in God and his promises of eternal life.

The individual who lives "according to the spirit" realizes the futility of the values of existence "according to the flesh" and devalues them. We are delivered from the tyranny and oppression of the world and the flesh, in order to gain the freedom of becoming children of God. Living "according to the flesh" is living in the world, for the world, and in rebellion against God; living "according to the spirit" is living in the world but for God. Inauthentic existence involves treating the world both as the place in which we live and as the bounds and norms of our existence; authentic existence involves treating the world as the place in which we live and God as the reason and basis of our existence. In other words, Christians are in the world but not of the world (John 17:6–19).

This point may be developed further with reference to John's Gospel. We have noted how "the world" can have two senses in relation to human existence: a *neutral* sense, meaning simply "the place in which we live" or "other human beings"; and a *negative* sense, meaning "a threat to our existence." In its negative sense, "the world" stands for the forces that threaten to overwhelm us and trap us through shackling us to things that are temporary, transient, and temporal. It is interesting to note that we find the same word used in these two senses in John's Gospel. Often, "the world" is used in its neutral sense— for example, in the famous affirmation, "God so loved the world that he gave his one and only Son, that whoever believes in him shall not perish but have eternal life" (John 3:16). More often, however (especially towards the end of the Gospel), "the world" assumes a negative sense, meaning "a threat to authentic Christian existence" (for example, John 15:18–19; 16:33). The world is increasingly seen as exerting a sinister influence upon faith, threatening to overwhelm it and pull the believer back into the world of tangible and material things from which he was called. The great theme of "victory over the world," which is so characteristic a feature of the later chapters of this Gospel, is primarily a victory over the threat to faith which the world poses. Similarly, Christians may be said to be in the world yet not of the world—meaning that Christians live in the world (the neutral sense of the term), but do not share the inauthentic existence which the world (in its negative sense) offers. This negative aspect of the world, however, is only fully recognized from the standpoint of faith, which recognizes the judgment passed upon that world by Jesus Christ.

The doctrine of justification by faith thus proclaims the possibility of the abolition of our alienation from our authentic mode of existence. It declares that we are offered as a gift an authentic mode of existence which we cannot attain by our own efforts. It offers to transform our existence so that, although we continue to remain in the world (for the time being), we are no longer oppressed by its values and threatened by the fear of death. God has overcome the world through Jesus Christ, and by overcoming it has set us free from its oppression (John 16:33), in order that we may live *in* it without being *of* it. The question of the authenticity of human existence troubles modern Western humanity as it has probably never troubled humanity before—and it is important to realize that the Christian doctrine addresses this question directly and offers its own characteristic solution. This is no outdated idea belonging to the museum of the history of ideas—it is an affirmation about the meaning and destiny of human existence that is as relevant today as it ever was.

5. *The Existential Point of Contact for the Gospel*

For generations, thinkers have tried to account for the strange and unhappy history of humanity—for the intractable fact of sin and human unhappiness. The less perceptive accounts of this problem attempt to externalize it by blaming the human predicament upon political and economic structures and other factors that are external to us. The more thoughtful and persuasive accounts of human misery, however, point to human nature itself as being the root of the problem—a problem that no amount of tinkering with economic and social structures will eliminate. The great French existentialist Albert Camus identified this problem in human nature as a profound alienation in our nature, a sense of lost innocence—in almost biblical terms he talks about the Fall and about a sense that we have been expelled from a homeland and are now unhappily wandering through history, trying to find a way to return. Where is that homeland? And how may we find it? Here we find a point of contact at the deepest level of human existence— the sense of *lostness*, of alienation, of inauthenticity.

The gospel proclamation is addressed to those who want their existence to be fulfilled and meaningful. It analyzes the existential situation of humanity, and then proceeds to describe the means by which the individual's situation may be transformed. Not very far from the surface of an individual's existence lie deep and dark fears about the threat of death and extinction and about the seeming meaninglessness of life. The gospel exposes these, bringing them to the surface in order that they may be faced and dealt with. For the gospel confronts the human fear of death and meaninglessness by speaking of someone who faced and conquered death, lending dignity and meaning to it. More importantly, the gospel treats the natural human desire to avoid dying and death and to seek refuge in the world as the symptom of human alienation from an authentic way of existence—in other words, fear of death and its corollaries are regarded as an aspect of the fundamental and global human alienation from God.

The gospel thus confirms what human *Angst* suggests—that there is something wrong with the way in which humanity exists. It also affirms that the human existential situation is capable of being transformed through acceptance and appropriation of what God has done for us in Jesus Christ. Something we could not achieve ourselves is offered to us. Earlier (p. 15) we noted an analysis of the human situation of value in contextualizing the gospel:

TABLE 1

Context of Experience	From	To	Through Jesus
Acceptance	Rejection	Acceptance	Love
Direction	to err about	to aim at	Call
Festival	Boredom	Joy	Feast-giver
Meaning	the absurd	the reasonable	Word
Liberation	Oppression	Liberation	Liberation
Becoming	Nobody	Somebody	Invitation
Fellowship	Solitude	Community	Presence

The gospel addresses each of these areas of existence. For example, the gospel addresses our feeling of existential rejection—the deep-seated feeling of "not being at home in the world" (Heidegger)—in order to tell us that we are accepted elsewhere by someone else. It teaches us to accept that we have been accepted by God, despite the fact that we are unacceptable. Our rejection by the world is thus transformed into our acceptance by God. The gospel addresses, and finds a point of contact in, our sense of not being right with or at home in the world—and interprets this in terms of our fulfillment, purpose, and destiny lying elsewhere. It speaks affirmatively of being accepted by God, of fulfillment and meaning being gained through responding to his love demonstrated in Jesus Christ. It speaks of us being *in* the world, but not *of* the world— identifying the world as our "playroom" (Heidegger), the area in which we exist, while locating the grounds of our fulfillment elsewhere.

This analysis could be extended to each of the remaining items on the above list. The category of "becoming" is of particular interest. The threat to human existence posed by death is that of ceasing to exist in any meaningful sense. We lose our identities. We become nobodies. Christianity doesn't talk about our individual identities being swallowed up into the absolute (like the Buddhist Nirvana), but about God affirming our identities in order to fulfill and perfect them. We become somebody. We stop living at the purely biological level (*bios*) and embrace life in all its fullness (*zoe*). The threats to our individual existence are overcome and disarmed. The Christian understanding of resurrection is of particular interest here, because of its emphasis on the continuity of personal identity after death. God affirms that we are somebody, that we mean much to him, and that to him our individual identity is distinct from everybody else's. The reader may like to extend this analysis to other items on the list.

Earlier we noted the important distinction between "objective" and "subjective" knowledge. The doctrine of justification by faith does not concern objective knowledge of "God in himself" (*Deus in se*), but the subjective knowledge of "God for us" (*Deus pro nobis*). The Christian proclamation, founded upon and embodying this doctrine, concerns *Deus iustificans* (Luther), a God who apprehends us, enters into our experience and transforms it, abolishing our alienation from our true existence in order that we might have and hold the glorious liberty of the children of God. "It is not we who handle these matters, but we who are handled by God" (Luther). Something that is beyond ourselves and our resources is *given* to us through grace and accepted by us through faith. So long as human beings walk the face of this earth, knowing that they must die, the gospel of authentic existence, of life in the midst of death, through the death and resurrection of Jesus Christ will continue to be exciting and relevant. Through the gospel proclamation we are presented with the possibility—as a gift!—of authentic human existence, living with God and for God, being forgiven and renewed through our acceptance of the crucified and risen Christ. This is indeed good news for humanity—and it is *intelligible* good news for modern Western humanity!

7   THE PERSONAL DIMENSION

Personal growth, personal development, personal relationships, and personal fulfillment are important items on the life
agendas of many today. Some of the major preoccupations of
contemporary society are linked with the idea of "the person"—preoccupations such as purpose and meaning. But what
does it mean to speak of a "person"? In what way does a
"person" differ from an "individual"? And in what way can the
Christian doctrine of justification by faith address this interest
in "the person"?

First, let us recall that Christians have found it natural and
helpful to think and speak of God as a person. The Old and
New Testaments alike continually ascribe to God attributes—
such as love, compassion, mercy, kindness, purpose, and
anger—that we naturally associate with persons. The idea of a
personal relationship between God and the individual believer,
established through the death and resurrection of Jesus Christ,
has long been recognized as an exceptionally helpful way of
understanding the way in which God deals with us. Thus Paul
is able to use the same verb ("to reconcile") to refer to both the
restoration of a wife to her estranged husband (1 Cor. 7:11) and
the restoration of the relationship between God and ourselves
through Jesus Christ (2 Cor. 5:18–20). Indeed, many contemporary Christian writers have gone further than this, emphasizing that to think of God in abstract, rather than personal, terms
(such as "power") is to lose sight of an essential aspect of the
nature of God.[1]

In an earlier chapter, we pointed out (p. 24) that the Old
Testament concept of "righteousness" is now generally regarded as being grounded in personal relationship: to be righteous

is to be faithful to a personal relationship. It implies acting upon the obligations, responsibilities, and privileges this relationship brings with it. For the Old Testament writers, the relationship in question was primarily the relationship between God and his people Israel. The related term "justification" can also bear this personal meaning and refer to the *rectification* of a personal relationship. To justify a person is to place him in the right relation to another person. It is this personal dimension of the doctrine of justification by faith that we shall explore in this chapter.

1. The Basics of Personalism

In recent years, there has been renewed interest in the idea of God as a "person." This interest may be traced to the writings of Martin Buber and the personalist philosophy he developed, usually referred to as "dialogical personalism."[2] This philosophy has proved to be of considerable importance in modern attempts to explain the nature of God and his dealings with humanity,[3] and in this chapter we propose to indicate its relevance for a contemporary understanding of the doctrine of justification by faith.

Buber points out that there are two basic ways in which we experience things, and designates one *experience* and the other *encounter*. To illustrate "experience," imagine a stone lying on a table, awaiting our inspection. We can look at the stone, we can pick it up and handle it, we can weigh it, and even send bits of it off to a laboratory for chemical analysis. The stone remains there, completely passive. It contributes nothing by way of self-disclosure, and it is we who have to engage in activity in order to gain a knowledge and understanding of it. First, we have to find the stone—it doesn't come looking for us! Then, once we have found it, we have to begin a long process of investigation to discover what it is like. The stone doesn't disclose this to us. We are active and the stone is passive throughout the relationship. Much the same is true of our relationship with most other living things—a tree, for example, or a fish. We *experience* them, in that they do not actively contribute to our attempts to know and understand them. Furthermore, the stone isn't changed by being experienced by us. It is still there, unchanged (unless, of course, a bit has been removed for chemical analysis). Because it does not *participate* in the relationship, it is not affected by it. As Buber pointed out, "The world does not participate in experience. It allows itself to be experienced, but it is not concerned, for it contributes nothing, and nothing happens to it."[4]

This point can be developed by making a distinction between an *object* and a *subject*. An object is something that is passive, that is available for our inspection, but that does not initiate disclosure. A subject, however, is someone who is active, who takes the initiative in knowing or understanding. Thus, going back to the example of the stone lying on the table, the stone can be said to be an *object*, while the person trying to gain knowledge of it can be said to be a *subject*. Buber designates this type of experience as an "I-It" relation—the sort of relationship which we have with a passive object.

Let us now contrast this with a very different example. Let us suppose that you are at a party, and you find yourself introduced to another person. What difference is there between that person and a stone? Four main areas of difference are immediately obvious. First, with the stone you had to take the initiative in knowing or understanding it—but with another person you may find that they take the initiative away from you! They may start trying to find out about *you* before you have a chance to start finding out about them. They may come looking for you before you start looking for them! Second, the stone was passive, and didn't disclose itself to you—you had to do all the hard work. But with another person, you may find that they start disclosing themselves to you. While you are still wondering how to start finding out about them, they may begin to tell you all about themselves. Third, there was no way that the stone would start trying to find out what you were like, but there is every chance that this other person may start quizzing you. You are addressed by someone else. With the stone, you were in the position of asking all the questions—but with another person, you may find that they are quizzing you while you are trying to quiz them. Fourth, the "It" is not changed by being experienced by us. The stone just remains the same. But a "You" may be changed by the encounter with an "I," just as the "I" may be changed by the encounter with a "You." The relation is potentially mutually transformative and creative. Both "I" and "You" contribute to and participate in the relationship: it is something reciprocal and mutual.

These four areas help define what Buber calls an "I-You" relationship. (English translations of Buber's works often designate this an "I-Thou" relationship, to emphasize that the "You" is singular rather than plural. This archaic phrase can be avoided, so long as it is remembered that the "You" in an "I-You" relationship is always a singular.) An "I-You" relationship is an *encounter* between two subjects, each of which actively contributes to the relationship. It is the fact that both subjects are active that distinguishes this relationship from an "I-It" experience in which only one of the two participants is active. The "You" can thus (1) take the initiative away from the "I"; (2) disclose himself to the "I"; (3) force the "I" to disclose himself; and (4) be changed by the "I"—and none of these are possibilities within the context of an "I-It" experience. Whereas we have control over an "It" and can dictate the course of our relationship with it, our relationship with another "You" is unpredictable, creative, and open. It can develop and change, and become something new and exciting.

2. *God as a Person*

As Buber pointed out, God must be treated as a "You," a subject we encounter rather than an object we experience. Many theologians have tended to treat God as some sort of object that human beings could discover by thinking hard or by studying culture, the world, or the stars. He was something over which we had control and whom we could seek out. To use Buber's terms, God was being treated as an "It"—while he should be treated as a "You." This point was developed by theologians such as Emil Brunner, who showed that the idea of "a personal God" embodies many of the essential biblical insights concerning the being and nature of God. The following points will help bring this out.

First, God must be recognized as having taken the initiative away from us by disclosing himself to us before we began to seek him. From beginning to end, Scripture witnesses to the gracious self-revelation of God rather than to human discovery of God or to rational proofs of his existence. God is known first and foremost as the God who reveals himself, who makes himself known, who discloses himself. God encounters us by addressing us, and this encounter with him is his gift (we shall return to this point shortly). We are not required to discover God but to respond to him as he has made himself known.

Second, "God" is not something we can examine at leisure under conditions of our own choosing. He is no stone on a table awaiting our examination and study. Rather, we must recognize that—like any other person—God is independent, with a will of his own, who allows us to encounter him on his own terms. As Buber pointed out, every "I-You" relationship is a *relationship of grace*, in that it presupposes that both the "I" and the "You" are *willing* to relate to each other. In order for a relationship to develop, both parties to that relationship must be willing to disclose themselves, and each must be prepared to allow the other to encounter him or her. God encounters us and discloses himself to us in a relationship of grace in that he is willing and prepared to disclose himself to us. To seek God elsewhere than in his gracious self-disclosure is to lose that encounter altogether and to treat God as an object.

Third, God has revealed himself primarily in personal form. God addresses us as persons in the form of a person. It is in the person of Jesus Christ, the "Word become flesh" (John 1:14), that we encounter the definitive self-revelation of God—and as that revelation is embodied in a person, it is both inevitable and right that we should think of God in personal terms. To those who suggest that this represents some sort of primitive anthropomorphism unsuitable for modern sophisticated humanity, it may be pointed out that this insight is far more sophisticated than the philosophical concepts of God they would have us adopt in its place. It points to personal relationships—the arena of the highest human values and most profound human feelings—as a model for our encounter with God. To speak of God as "love" is immediately to speak of the supreme human experience of love as giving insights into the nature of God. And if the idea of "love" is too unsophisticated for some, it may surely be reasonably suggested that their sophistication is preventing them from encountering the deepest experience of reality open to us in this life!

It will therefore be clear that to speak of God as a person is to remain faithful to a number of central and essential biblical insights into the nature of God. It is now appropriate to ask how the insights of dialogical personalism may be applied to the doctrine of justification by faith.

The essential point that must be made is that the doctrine of justification may be recast in terms of personal relationships. Whereas some of the language traditionally used in connection with the doctrine of justification (such as "imputation," "forensic," and so forth) is unfamiliar to many, the idea of a personal relationship is familiar to everyone from their own experience. All of us are involved with other persons and relate to them. All of us are familiar with the way in which relationships begin and develop (and end), whether from our own experience, from reading books, or from watching the latest television soap opera. An immediate point of contact is established with human experience. To drop into jargon for a moment: the categories of personal experience are receptor-oriented towards Western culture, and the perceptive theologian, teacher, or preacher is in r ` excellent position to exploit this point of contact in order onvey the insights of the gospel in this way.

3. Personal Relationships

It will be clear from the discussion so far that a *person* is basically an *individual who is involved in relationships*. In other words, the idea of a person suggests a network of relationships with other persons. An individual is solitary, but a person exists in relationships with others. Now let us ask how a relationship between two persons begins. First, we note the point made by Buber—both these persons are *subjects*. In other words, they are both active in their relationships with the world and other persons and are able to exercise near-total control over their relationships with passive objects, and a certain degree of control over their relationships with other active subjects. With this point in mind we may consider how a personal relationship is initiated. Let us consider John and

Mary. Initially, they do not know each other. Then they meet, and John takes the initiative in introducing himself to Mary. What happens next? A number of possibilities exist.

1. John and Mary interact, and get to know something about each other. They discover that they have a common interest in the novels of Betty McDonald. John would like this relationship to develop further, but Mary feels that she would like to keep the relationship on the Betty McDonald level.
2. John and Mary interact, and get to know something about each other. They discover that they have a mutual interest in flowers: John runs a seed import business and Mary has earned a master's degree in flower arranging at an until recently famous midwestern university. Mary indicates that she would like "a meaningful on-going relationship to develop," at which point John decides that he isn't into academics. The relationship does not develop.
3. John and Mary interact, and get to know something about each other. They discover that they have no particular interests in common, but that they *are* interested in each other. A relationship develops as a result.

In situations (1) and (2), no relationship results, although in both cases moves are initiated that might lead to a relationship. But in neither case are John and Mary prepared to allow this to take place. They are both able to exercise control over the situation to the extent that they prevent any relationship from developing. They come to learn *about* each other, but not to *know* each other. In effect, they treat each other as an "It." Essential to the idea of the person is the freedom to enter into a relationship with other persons: to deny this freedom is to stop treating this individual as a *person* and start treating him as a *thing*—an *object* that has no say in its destiny. Only in situation (3) are both John and Mary willing to allow a relationship to develop.

The theological application of this is obvious. God takes the initiative in encountering us through the word of proclamation, disclosing himself to us. This is an act of sheer grace—God is under no obligation to us to do any such thing, yet he does so out of his love for us. God makes himself available to us in a personal manner, entering into our experience and meeting us where we are. He addresses us, he calls us, he offers us his friendship. God proclaims his love for us, in word and in deed. God condescends to enter into a relationship with his creatures. But it takes two to make a personal relationship, and unless we say "Yes!" to God, that relationship remains unfulfilled. God has given us the immense privilege of saying "No!" to him. God treats us as persons, not as objects. Our decisions, our feelings, matter to him and are respected by him.

This point is of particular importance in relation to the doctrine of universal salvation, which has gained some following in modern theological circles but is, in fact, based on a sub-Christian view of God.

4. Universalism and Personalism

One challenge to the relevance of the doctrine of justification by faith arises from the suggestion that *all* human beings will eventually be saved—a doctrine usually known as *universalism*. According to this doctrine, the love of God for humanity is such that every human being will eventually be saved. God expresses his love for humanity by condemning none and saving all. In many respects, this is an appealing doctrine, particularly to those attracted by the Enlightenment view that all religions possess essentially the same validity. It will be obvious that if this doctrine is correct, the doctrine of justification by faith loses its power and relevance: since all will be saved anyway, there is not much point in proclaiming salvation and the conditions upon which it is made available. But is this doctrine *right*? Although superficially attractive, the doctrine is in fact deeply offensive and harsh. It parallels Pelagianism in this respect (see pp. 39–44): although seeming to be reasonable and positive, it is actually intensely authoritarian and continually threatens to compromise humanity's God-given integrity. Let us consider why this is the case.

Such is the respect that God has for us, that we are given the enormous privilege of being able to say "No!" to God. It is this, after all, that distinguishes a person from an object, a "You" from an "It." The offer of forgiveness, renewal, and transformation is there, waiting for us to accept it—but we are not coerced to accept it. In John's Gospel, we read of Jesus encountering an invalid and taking pity upon him. "Do you want to get well?" he asked this unfortunate individual (John 5:56). The offer was there, but the decision to accept or reject it remained the invalid's.

This privilege of saying "No!" to God must be respected. One of the greatest travesties of this privilege—indeed, one of the greatest travesties of human dignity—is precisely this doctrine of "universalism." According to this doctrine, everyone will eventually be saved. They may not wish to be saved, but they have no say in the matter. Whether they like it or not, everyone will receive eternal life. Those who hold this doctrine usually protest against what they term the "exclusivism" of the gospel—the suggestion that some are deliberately excluded from eternal life—as compromising human dignity. And, totally unwittingly, they thus compromise the very human dignity that they treat with such respect. What happens, we may reasonably ask, if someone doesn't want to be saved? After all, it is perfectly obvious that at least a substantial part of the human population would regard the idea of being cooped up with God for eternity as something to be avoided at any cost!

But let us develop this point further. Let us suppose that one individual does not want to be saved. Unless the universalist denies human free will, this possibility must be acknowledged as genuine. *At least one* individual, and almost certainly a number several orders of magnitude greater, will not wish to be saved. What will God do about it? According to traditional Christian teaching, as expressed in the New Testament and elsewhere, God will respect that decision. God wants everyone to be saved—but, in the end, will not force himself upon an individual who, through exercise of his God-given freedom, decides that he does not wish to fulfill his relationship with his creator and redeemer. But for the universalist, God must *force* this individual to be saved. He must violate this individual's freedom and integrity. The same free will God gave to this individual is overruled as God gets his way and ignores the wishes of the individual. In an insulting display of paternalism, universalism represents God as brushing aside and overruling the wishes of the individual on the grounds that he knows best what is right for that person. To put this very crudely, but accurately: where traditional Christianity speaks of God seeking a free response of love on the part of the individual towards him, universalism is obliged to represent God as *raping* this individual. No choice is offered, and the integrity of that individual is totally compromised. Rape involves treating a *person* as an *object*—and that is precisely what is happening in this unthinkable scene.

This is not the view of traditional Christianity, which knows of a God who offers himself to us and is deeply wounded by our rejection of him—but who nevertheless respects our decision. God continually treats us as *persons*, not as *objects*. For the decision to accept or reject God remains *our* decision, a decision for which we and we alone are responsible. God gives us every assistance possible to make the decision he wants us to make, but he cannot make that decision for us. God enables us to accept his offer of forgiveness and renewal by removing or disarming every obstacle in its path—obstacles such as spiritual blindness, arrogance, confusion, a compromised freedom of the will, and so forth. But, in the end, God cannot and does not make that decision for us. To affirm human dignity is to affirm our ability to say "No!" to God—an affirmation the New Testament and the Christian tradition have no hesitation in making. Universalism perverts the gospel of the love of God into an obscene scene of theological rape quite unworthy of the God whom we encounter in the face of Jesus Christ.

God offers us a personal relationship with him through grace—and if that relationship is to be fulfilled, we must accept it. The doctrine of justification by faith affirms that it is God who takes the initiative and we who respond to that initiative. But personal relationships are not static—they are dynamic, they *develop*, they *change individuals*. And so our relationship with God, once established, forms the context within which we develop. It is the starting point for becoming more like the God who has entered into this gracious relationship with us. All of us know how the two parties in a relationship become closer as that relationship matures and develops. And so it is with our personal relationship with God. It is a transformational relationship, in which our knowledge of God deepens and we become more like him. There is no such thing as a "legal fiction" in the area of personal relations! Saying "Yes!" to God is opening the way to a dynamic and transforming relationship in which God meets us where we are and takes us on from there to become like him.

5. Original Sin and Personalism

This personalist approach to the doctrine of justification by faith is particularly helpful in relation to two areas: the doctrine of original sin, and the relationship between creation and redemption. Scripture does not see the relationship between God and humanity established through the death and resurrection of Jesus Christ as being the initiation of a new relationship, but rather as the restoration of an old one. The relationship established between God and his creations in the action of creation and broken through the Fall is reestablished through the death and resurrection of Christ. Yet even in its fallen state, humanity remains the creature of God. How are we to distinguish between the fallen and redeemed states, since humanity remains the creature of God in both cases?

The personalist answer to this important question can be illustrated particularly well from the parable of the prodigal son (Luke 15:11–32). Of the three parables linked together in Luke 15 to illustrate the idea of lostness it is this one that has captured the imagination of generations. Perhaps we all know this parable too well to appreciate its vividness and clarity. Perhaps we all too easily concentrate upon the wayward son and overlook the tender picture of the waiting father, watching for the return of his son. Every age has its "distant country" (Luke 15:13), its own form of lostness, and can see its own predicament poignantly reflected in the narrative of the proud adventurer turned into repentant refugee. The son journeys to the distant land, there to be treated and exploited as an object. His assertion of his independence from his father eventually leads to the loss of his identity as a person, as he becomes merely a lost individual in a foreign land. And then he remembers his relationship with his father, in which he was treated and loved as a person.

Throughout the moving narrative, however, the son remains what he is—the son of his father. Nothing can destroy that relationship: it is something that is "given," something the son tries to cast off but eventually reclaims. The son may act as if he were *not* the son of his father, the relationship may be purely *nominal*; nevertheless, it remains. The son has no other father. Nothing will alter the fact that the father has this specific and unique relation to his son. As the son journeys into that distant country, his father becomes a memory, a past event; he is experienced as an "It," rather than a "You." But the relationship remains there, as real as it is unacknowledged. The great turning point in that parable (Luke 15:18–19) is when the son reclaims the relationship, making once again actual what had become nominal, and recognizing his father as a "You" rather than an "It": he arises and goes back to encounter his father, to reclaim and restore that relationship. The relation of the father to the son is still there, as it was before and would be after—but the son is now prepared to make that relation real and vital, rather than nominal and dead.

The theological significance of this point will be obvious. All of humanity are the children of God, but that relationship is experienced in purely nominal terms, if it is experienced at all. God is experienced as an "It", if at all. Humanity may be created in the image of God, just as the prodigal son is created after the likeness of his father—but humanity, like that prodigal son, experiences God as little more than a haunting and distant memory, a faint melody from a distant and unreachable land, the scent of a strange and far-off blossom. But the relationship is there. It can be reclaimed and restored. God can become a "You" and not an "It." God can be encountered as we return to meet him, not merely experienced in a distant and ambiguous manner.

To put this in more theological terms, we can say that humanity has fallen and is alienated from God—but through the death and resurrection of Jesus Christ the possibility of reconciliation to God is proclaimed. Whether alienated from God or reconciled to him, humanity remains the creature of God. But in the former case the relationship is purely nominal—in all that humanity says and does it denies that it is the creature of God. Genesis 3 makes it clear that the fundamental sin of humanity lies in denying its creaturely status and attempting to become self-sufficient, placing itself in the place of God its creator. But through the reconciling death and resurrection of Jesus Christ, appropriated by faith, humanity is able to transform that nominal relationship into a real relationship, acknowledging the fact that it is God's creature and joyfully accepting the rights and responsibilities this brings with it, as humanity "is brought into the glorious freedom of the children of God" (Rom. 8:21).

This discussion illustrates the deficiency of the view that humanity is adequately defined *theologically* in terms of being "the creature of God." It will be obvious that the distinctively *Christian* understanding of humanity is that of "a creature of God *who requires redemption through Jesus Christ.*" To say that an individual is a "creature of God" says nothing about the actual status of that relationship. It is as meaningful as defining the prodigal son as "the son of the father": this is *true*, but inadequate—it does not allow us to make the crucial distinction between the *alienated* and *reconciled* states of that son! To be unable to distinguish between the son as he tends to pigs on a distant foreign soil and that same son as he rushes to embrace his waiting and forgiving father is not merely to miss the point of a splendid parable—it is to miss the point of the gospel altogether!

It will also be clear that the concept of original sin may be illuminated by thinking of it in personalist terms, in terms of a broken personal relationship. Original sin is the state of existing in a broken relationship, alienated from the true way of existence. It is to live in a distant land, with only the haunting and fading memory of the homeland. It is like living in the aftermath of the break-up of a personal relationship. It is the state of being alienated from a friend. So deep is that alienation and so distant is the memory of him that, to all intents and purposes, God might as well not exist. And it is to *this* situation that the gospel proclamation of the possibility of restoration is addressed. God has taken the initiative in offering us reconciliation, offering to restore the relationship to what it once was and what it was always meant to be. The sense of joy is similar to that which greeted the news that Jerusalem's period of

Babylonian captivity was to be ended, as God restored his people to their former relationship with him:

> How beautiful upon the mountains are the feet of those who bring good news, who proclaim peace, who bring good tidings, who proclaim salvation, who say to Zion, "Your God reigns!" Listen! Your watchmen lift up their voices; together they shout for joy. When the Lord returns to Zion, they will see it with their own eyes. Burst into songs of joy together, you ruins of Jerusalem, for the Lord has comforted his people, he has redeemed Jerusalem (Isa. 52:7–9).

The gospel proclamation interprets *human experience of the absence of God* as *experience of alienation from God* and proclaims that this alienation may be abolished through accepting the offer of reconciliation and forgiveness that God extends to us. This offer remains an offer of sheer grace—nothing that we could do or have done deserves what God chooses to do out of his overwhelming love for us. Unilaterally, God takes the initiative in coming to us, in entering into our history and our experience, in order to meet us and address us with the word of forgiveness and reconciliation. To use Buber's terms, God ceases to be an "It" and becomes a "You." We cease to *experience* him as absent or far away and *encounter* him as our Lord and Savior.

6. The Personalist Point of Contact for the Gospel

How may these personalist insights help us address the doctrine of justification by faith to the contemporary Western human situation? The modern Western preoccupation with personal relationships and categories such as "personal fulfillment" allows a gospel that speaks of a personal encounter with God, of the fulfillment of human personality, to be grounded in the contemporary situation. As we shall see in a moment, human relationships are not fulfilling in themselves but point beyond themselves to the ground of their fulfillment—and the Christian doctrine of justification asserts that the ground of their fulfillment is none other than the living

God, who makes himself available to us. We begin reflecting upon the curious sense of bitter-sweet longing associated with human personal relationship by considering a musical analogy. Suppose you are listening to a remarkable musical work— perhaps Beethoven's *Eroica* symphony, or a Wagner opera. As you listen to it, you are aware that through the medium of the music comes a person—the person of the composer, who is reaching you and involving you in his personal engagement with the forces of fate and destiny. You are caught up with his passions and concerns as you listen to his music and attempt to understand it. The music mediates the person—it points beyond itself to its ground and basis in the person of its composer. Something—such as the sense of *Sturm und Drang* in a Brahms symphony, or the deep sense of melancholy in Tchaikovsky's *Pathétique*—comes *through* the music even though it is not actually *in* the music. And as we try to capture that sense, we find that it eludes us: it lies beyond our reach— something has been evoked but cannot be grasped. This same sense of something that is so nearly captured and yet eludes us is a characteristic feature of human relationships.

In human personal relationships is to be found a parable of our need for God. In love, the deepest human relationship of all, we encounter the strange longing to lose ourselves in another—to enter into a relationship that, paradoxically, simultaneously heightens and obliterates our own identity. We do not just love something *about* another—such as an interest in the literary works of Betty McDonald or flower arranging—but we love *another*. We love them for what they are, as persons. This is the stuff of personal relationships, the need for another person, a "You" whom we may encounter. Yet somehow in personal relationships there is to be found a bitter-sweet longing—something that comes *through* the relationship but is not *in* that relationship. It is as if a personal relationship points to something beyond itself, something that Buber calls "the eternal You." The paradox of hedonism—the simple yet stultifying fact that pleasure cannot satisfy—is another instance of this curious phenomenon. Pleasure, beauty, personal relationships—all seem to promise so much, and yet when we grasp them we find that what we were seeking was not located in them, but lies beyond them. The great English literary critic and theologian C. S. Lewis captured this insight perfectly:

> The books or the music in which we thought the beauty was located will betray us if we trust in them; it was not *in* them, it only came *through* them, and what came through them was longing. These things—the beauty, the memory of our own past—are good images of what we really desire; but if they are mistaken for the thing itself they turn into dumb idols, breaking the hearts of their worshippers. For they are not the thing itself; they are only the scent of a flower we have not found, the echo of a tune we have not heard, news from a country we have not visited.[5]

Our existence and experience as persons—whether it be of other persons, of beauty, or of pleasure—point beyond, like signposts, to something they themselves can never capture or encapsulate.

One of the most sensuously stimulating works of recent English literature is Evelyn Waugh's novel *Brideshead Revisited*, which captures the frustration of so much personal experience, whether in the quest for love or the quest for beauty. Somehow that quest always falls to find its object. Even when the search seems close to its end, we find another corner to turn:

> Perhaps all our loves are merely hints and symbols; vagabond-language scratched on gateposts and paving-stones along the weary road that others have tramped before us; perhaps you and I are types and this sadness which sometimes falls between us springs from disappointment in our search, each straining through and beyond the other, snatching a glimpse now and then of the shadow, which turns the corner always a pace or two ahead of us.[6]

And have we not been told, and probably discovered to our cost, that "it is better to journey in hope than to arrive," a theme so beautifully crafted into story form in John Master's classic novel *Coromandel*?

It is here that we may begin to ground the Christian doctrine of justification: in the experience of longing, of the constant failure to capture something that seems to be there in a personal relationship, pointing beyond it, but that seems to be forever beyond our grasp. As Buber points out, every human "You" points beyond itself to "the eternal You," to God. The unfulfilled dimension of a human relationship points to God: what is conveyed through human relationships, but not in them, makes itself—makes *himself*—available to us as a gift.

This curious feature of longing, of reaching out for what seems to be within our grasp, parallels the situation of the prodigal son. Even in the distant country he remembers the homeland. Its distant echo reverberates within him. It is as if we were born in a distant country, yet remembering our homeland. Traces and hints of that homeland are all around us, beckoning us, inviting us to grasp them—and yet we can never reach out and possess them. We see and hear them through, but not in, others. It is this point of contact that the gospel of justification addresses. The "It" we know intuitively to lie through and beyond our quests and hopes discloses himself as a "You." We learn that our longings point to something, to some*one*, whom we were longing for. "What you worship as something unknown, I am going to proclaim to you" (Acts 17:23).

The gospel thus complements and develops such insights by proclaiming the astonishing insight that a *person* lies behind and under our personal existence—and more than that: it is possible to *relate* to this person, to the "You" who lies beyond and behind every human "I-You" relationship. God discloses himself in personal form, in order to enter into a relationship with us, in which our own personality is both heightened and obliterated—as in any deep personal relationship. God takes the initiative in the process that leads to the fulfillment of our personal potential—by relating to the person, "the eternal You," who underlies our personal experience. To encounter God is to encounter what every personal relationship seems to promise yet fails to deliver.

The doctrine of justification by faith addresses the human need for the fulfillment of personality and affirms that God has made himself available for us, as a person, in order that we might become the persons we are destined to be. Justification is about the transformation and fulfillment of our persons through an encounter with *the* Person who underlies personality itself. It affirms a right and a wrong way in which this may be done: "Seek God—or, rather, recognize that he has sought you out and found you—and you will find personal fulfillment and purpose. But seek personal fulfillment and purpose, and you will find that they elude you, slipping through your fingers when you thought you had found them." For the doctrine of justification by faith reminds us that these are things that we ourselves cannot achieve but are graciously given to us by God, who asks us to receive them from his hands. True personality and authentic existence—which judge our ideas of "true" personality and "authentic" existence and find them wanting— are both offered to us by God through Jesus Christ.

The personalist approach to the doctrine of justification by faith thus makes a direct appeal to our experience of personal relationships and shows how these may be transformed. It speaks to us of a God who takes the initiative in addressing us and in offering us the possibility of a renewed and restored personal relationship with us. It remains faithful to the central biblical insights into the personal nature and purposes of God, and to the simple fact, so eloquently witnessed to in Scripture and so powerfully confirmed through Christian experience, that God does not encounter us as an idea, concept, or argument—but as a person.

8   THE ETHICAL DIMENSION

The Christian church and the Christian believer exist in the world and are required to live and act within it. But what principles and presuppositions should govern and guide the way in which Christians act within both the believing community and society? The Christian can hardly be expected to behave in exactly the same manner as his non-Christian neighbor and endorse each and every moral belief of secular society. In recent decades there has been a growing interest in the field of Christian ethics, and this growth shows no sign of abating. Ethics is widely regarded as embodying the practical or pragmatic aspect of Christian theology, with a contemporary relevance denied to Christian theology itself. But what is the relationship between ethics and theology in particular, and ethics and Christian faith in general? In this chapter we propose to demonstrate how the doctrine of justification by faith lays a sound foundation for the development of a distinctively and authentically *Christian* ethical system. It is at the point of ethical decision-making that Christian theology is seen by outsiders as coming out of the ghetto of the church and taking root in the world in which others live, thus establishing the interface between faith and unbelief.

For those who feel that the Christian church should establish its identity and relevance in the eyes of the world by its actions, the temptation is thus always there to treat ethics as the chief or sole aspect of Christianity. The rapid growth of "secular Christianity" prior to its equally rapid fall was marked by the belief that the secular justification of Christianity lay in the field of concrete political and social action, while matters of doctrine were seen as being at best peripheral and at worst a positive hindrance to establishing the relevance of the gospel in the modern period. Much was made of "Christianity come of age"—a faith without religion and belief, which was committed to socially acceptable political action. Inevitably, however, a critical attitude developed towards these trends. On what basis could the acceptability of such actions be judged? The church could hardly be expected to say "Amen!" to each and every contemporary attitude! The increasing recognition of the ethical shallowness and superficiality of secular "undogmatic" Christianity led to a growing concern to establish the basis upon which responsible, critical, *Christian* ethical decision-making could proceed. One of the most remarkable indicators of this change in mood was the increasing interest shown in Europe in the theology of Karl Barth, which, it was realized, established a basis for a Christian ethics—whereas the thought of Paul Tillich, once thought so relevant, was increasingly recognized as devoid of ethical significance.[1]

1. Theology and Ethics

Christian ethics must not be regarded as that compartment or division of Christian theology which attempts to work out the practical consequences of that theology. Christian faith is the root and ground of both Christian theology and Christian ethics. The question addressed by Christian theology is how our faith expresses itself in the way we think, while the question addressed by Christian ethics is how our faith should express itself in the practical affairs of human life. Just as theology deals with the question of how Christian faith affects the way we think about God, ourselves, and the world, so Christian ethics deals with the question of how we should act in that world. Ethics and theology are thus concerned with the unfolding of faith, and both must be regarded as essential to the life of the Christian church.[2] The Christian church must *think* and must *act* on the basis of its faith—and that thinking and acting are not independent of each other, but are related in the closest of manners. Both derive from faith in Jesus Christ as Lord and Savior, and this faith must find its expression in thought and deed.

It is as impossible to reduce Christian faith to matters of ethics as it is to suggest that ethics are irrelevant to Christian life: precisely because believers think and act, the permanent relevance and mutual relationship of Christian theology and ethics must be recognized. It may be, of course, that at certain moments in history it proves necessary to emphasize the ethical dimension of Christianity, just as at others it may prove necessary to dwell upon its doctrinal aspects—but this must be recognized as a tactical development, based upon the perceived needs of the moment, rather than as a permanent and irreversible development within Christianity. The mistake made with such astonishing ease by "secular Christianity" was to treat a short-term shift in attitudes as if it were a permanent development.

2. The Transformation of the Situation of the Moral Agent

The doctrine of justification by faith establishes the mutual relationship of faith, theology, and ethics in terms of the redeeming and transforming encounter of the living God with the sinner as an individual. The *gift* of our justification lays upon us the *obligation* to live in accordance with our new status.[3] We are *made* children of God through our justification as an act of free grace—and now we must act in accordance with this transformation. The slogan "Become what you are!" neatly summarizes this situation and encapsulates the essence of Pauline ethics with some brilliance. In justification we are made to be the light of the world (Matt. 5:15–16): therefore we must shine out as lights in a dark world, as a city on a hill (v. 14; Phil. 2:15). Our justification brings about a new obedience—an obedience that would not be conceivable before our justification and that ultimately rests on the grace of God.

The significance of the gospel for ethics lies not so much in its answers to the focal questions of secular ethics (What must I do? And how can I know what I am meant to do?) as in its transforming of the situation of the moral agent. The focus and emphasis are shifted from what is to be done (the *agendum*) to the agent, to the one who is required to act. The presupposition of Christian ethics is precisely this transformation of the moral agent in conversion, and the inauguration of the "new obedience" through the renewing and regenerating action of the Holy Spirit. It is this alteration in the life and existence of the individual that establishes the point of departure for any authentically *Christian* ethical thinking; a failure to recognize and uphold this intimate relation between conversion and the new obedience opens the way to the reduction of the glorious liberty of the children of God to a mere external observance of rules and regulations.

In what sense is Christian ethics dependent upon Jesus Christ? Are Christians obliged to imitate the example of Christ in each and every area of life? The New Testament does not seem to understand Christian ethics as an "imitation of Christ." Jesus is not understood as an ethical pioneer who hacked his way through a moral jungle in order to make it easier for those who followed him. Rather, it is the cross and resurrection of Jesus Christ that are understood to constitute the very basis of the Christian life and Christian ethics alike. To follow Jesus is not so much to imitate his example in every respect as to participate in the salvation he accomplished for us. We do not become the children of God by imitating the Son of God, but we imitate the Son of God because we already *are* the children of God on account of what Jesus Christ accomplished through his death and resurrection, which we appropriate by faith. What God has done for us in Jesus Christ assumes a specific form in history that gives some shape, expression, and form to what human purposes and actions are appropriate expressions of "following Christ," but our interest in the example of Christ must ultimately be recognized to be a *consequence* rather than a *cause* of our justification by faith.

The New Testament is dominated by the proclamation of the transformation of sinful human beings through a redeeming encounter with the living God. This transformation is understood to be partial rather than total—something is initiated, or *inaugurated*, within us that will eventually be completed and fulfilled on the last day, but that has effects upon us here and now. A new situation in our personal existence is inaugurated through the gracious action of God. And this alteration in our situation leads to a new desire to obey God. It is God's gift that leads to the obligation on our part: the death and resurrection of Jesus Christ are the acts of God that bring into being a new covenant with consequential obligations for us as the covenant partners of God. This new desire to obey God, which before our conversion was either absent or present only to a diminutive extent, is now stimulated and catalyzed by the action of God within us, as a transformation in our outlook upon and understanding of life takes place. The New Testament uses helpful biological analogies to bring this point out.

In the Sermon on the Mount, Jesus points out that a good tree bears good fruit, and a bad tree bad fruit (Matt. 7:16–18). The nature of the fruit is biologically determined: grapes don't grow on thornbushes, nor do figs grow on thistles. These are the biological facts of life—if you want to get figs, you must grow a fig tree. Underlying this remarkably simple analogy is a profound theological insight: The transformation of humanity is a prerequisite for its reformation. Or, as Martin Luther put it, "It isn't good works which makes an individual good, but a good individual who does good works."

Luther develops this point with a number of useful analogies. For example, consider an apple tree in an orchard in the spring. We could go to that orchard and read numerous learned botanical textbooks to the tree, which inform it that it ought to bear apples in the fall. But the reason why the apple tree finally bears those apples in the fall is simply that it is an apple tree, and this is what apple trees do naturally. Similarly, Luther points out, Christians do not need to be told to do good works, because they do them naturally. Secondly, Luther points out that doing the sorts of things a bishop does—like dedicating churches or confirming children—doesn't make someone a bishop! The office precedes the function—otherwise an actor could dress up as a bishop and make himself into a bishop by doing the sorts of things a bishop usually does. *Because* an individual is a validly ordained bishop he may dedicate churches. And so Luther points out that it is the transformation of the situation of the moral agent through his justification by faith that initiates a process that leads to the performance of good works as a matter of course. To exhort a sinner to become good through his own works is about as realistic as telling a thornbush to bear grapes or a thistle to bear figs.

A contemporary illustration of this insight may be found in

the Oxford Group, founded in England in the 1920s by Frank Buchman and subsequently renamed Moral Rearmament (MRA). Buchman's emphasis on the Four Absolutes (absolute honesty, absolute purity, absolute unselfishness, and absolute love) made a deep impression on many and challenged them to undertake a personal moral revolution. Thus at the University of Cambridge, especially in the years 1929–32, the movement emphasized the distinction between "orthodoxy" and "life." What they had to offer was not any orthodox theology but the promise of new life through personal moral renewal. In practice, that personal moral renewal tended to be ephemeral. It had nothing to sustain it and in itself seemed incapable of giving new life. Indeed, the history of thought suggests that such moral renewal movements are remarkably short-lived; they tend to spring up like seed on rocky ground, only to die for lack of firm roots. The Christian affirms that new life leads to personal moral renewal, inverting the MRA order.

There is simply no point in informing sinful humanity that the world would be a better place if everyone stopped doing things that are wrong! What is required is a transformation of the human situation so that the motivation for doing wrong is reduced or eliminated. Humanity doesn't need moral education—it has had plenty over the last several thousand years and cannot really be said to be much the better off as a result. It seems to be a universal fact of human experience that when we attempt to live up to our moral ideals, we find ourselves failing in the attempt. We all recognize the claims of morality, and we find ourselves failing in the attempt to live up to them. Underlying both the view that the human predicament arises from ignorance and the view that Jesus Christ is nothing more than a good teacher is a remarkably shallow understanding of the nature of humanity itself. As the great American moral theologian Reinhold Niebuhr emphasized, all too many modern thinkers have tended to work with a remarkably naive view of human nature—probably reflecting the fact that their middle-class intellectual backgrounds tend to inhibit them from encountering and experiencing the darker side of human nature.

Of the many remarkable works relating to practical matters written by English Puritans, one of the most fascinating is

William Romaine's tract *A Method for Preventing the Frequency of Robbers and Murders*, published in London in 1770. In this work, Romaine pointed out that the law of the land was inadequate to deal with the root cause of robbery and murder. At best, it could inhibit them by prescribing severe penalties for those who were apprehended. Romaine pointed out that these measures were simply means of containing, rather than eliminating, the problem. The real problem lay in the sinful condition of humanity, which the legislature could merely control, rather than cure. The real solution lay in the transformation of human nature so that the individual was enabled to exercise at least some degree of control over that nature. And it is the gospel alone that holds the cure for the sinful condition of humanity:

> Thro' the merits of our Lord Jesus Christ, the divine grace and influence are offered unto us again, and whoever seeks them by humility and prayer, until he receive them, is then made a partaker of the Spirit of God, who first makes the heart faithful and penitent, and afterwards sanctifies it by the blood of Jesus Christ. . . . And whoever is renewed after the image of the second Adam, he has a clean and pure heart, and a sweet fountain might as soon send forth poisonous water, as this sanctified heart can produce murder, adultery, fornication, or any of the filthy works of the flesh.[4]

While we may find ourselves slightly amused at Romaine's optimism in trying to persuade the English legislature to encourage the preaching of the gospel, we must allow that he was making a serious and valid theological point. The law curbs human sinfulness by making it more difficult for it to indulge itself—but it does not cure it. Human regeneration, which brings about at least a partial transformation of our sinful nature, is required if the root cause is to be dealt with. As an Irishman, I can still remember hearing stories of a local Irish religious revival in the year 1859. One of its most significant side effects was that the local police force found themselves without a job to do, due to the sudden decline in the local crime rates!

There is thus an "automatic" or "natural" connection between the justification of the sinner and his desire and ability to perform good works. The New Testament analogy of the tree and its fruits expresses the fundamental idea that the radical transformation of the individual ("radical" comes from the Latin *radix*, meaning "root") is prior to his ability to produce good works. The New Testament, particularly the Pauline writings, emphasizes that this is to be understood as *God's transformation of us*, rather than as our own attempt to transform us. Thus Paul speaks of the "fruit of the Spirit" (Gal. 5:22), drawing attention to the fact that this "fruit" is the result of God's action within us, rather than our action independent of God. Therefore, whereas secular ethical systems tend to discuss moral acts in terms of their goal (in other words, what they achieve or are intended to achieve), a theological ethical system based on the doctrine of justification will discuss moral acts in terms of what they *presuppose* or *are intended to express*—the individual's radical transformation through his conversion. The starting point of an authentically *Christian* ethics is the recognition that the conversion of the individual inaugurates a new obedience, a new lifestyle, and a new ethic that is at least potentially different from secular ethical systems.

3. Ethics and Original Sin

The doctrine of justification forces us to acknowledge a determinative aspect of human nature that secular ethical systems tend to ignore, play down, or deny: sin. The fact that we are made in the image and likeness of God (Gen. 1:26–27) is a starting point for any discussion of our relationship with and responsibility towards God—and functions as precisely such a starting point in Jewish, Islamic, and Deist ethical systems. But for the Christian it is *only* a starting point in that it is necessary to recognize that, although we are created in the image of God, this image has become obscured, corrupted, and tarnished through sin. We are sinners—and any ethical system that fails to take the sinfulness of humanity with full seriousness must have its right to call itself "Christian" challenged.

The radical realism of the biblical view of sin and its

devastating consequences for our understanding of human beings as moral agents are captured in the words of Robert Browning in "Gold Hair":

'Tis the faith that launched point-blank its dart
At the head of a lie; taught Original Sin,
The corruption of man's heart.

The bland assumption of the natural and fundamental goodness of human nature, so characteristic of much Western liberal thought, is called into question by this doctrine. The myth of human perfectability and inevitable progress has been shown up for what it is by the savagery and cruelty of the twentieth century. If ever there has been a period in human history when human evil was evident, it is the twentieth century. How many outrages such as Auschwitz must we experience before the naive assumption that all human beings act out of the best of intentions is exposed for what it is—a cruel and seductive lie? Reason is so often used as a tool for human ends, rather than a guide to those ends. As Reinhold Niebuhr so provocatively stated this point: "The will to power uses reason, as kings use chaplains and courtiers, to add grace to their enterprises."[5]

4. Towards a Pragmatic Ethics

As we saw in connection with Augustine and the Pelagian controversy (pp. 33–45), the concept of original sin entails a human bias towards sin. In other words, there is something about human nature that inclines it to commit sin. It is not simply a matter of committing sin without knowing that we are doing so—it is, rather, *knowing* as we do so that we are sinning. We know what is right and what is required of us—and yet there is an inherent tendency to fail to live up to these ideals. All too many ethical systems adopt a very shallow and superficial approach to the human dilemma, precisely because they are based on the assumption that the basic human problem is simply the need to be told what is right and what is wrong—whereas this is only *part* of the problem! The real problems arise when we try to put into action what we know to be right and find ourselves failing to meet up to our ideals. Any ethical system that fails to recognize this dialectic between obligation and ability must be regarded as failing to encapsulate adequately a fundamental Christian insight into the nature of the human ethical agent. The congenital weakness of human nature is the submerged rock on which the naive claims of optimistic liberal thought founder so cruelly and so totally. The history of social ethics is littered with confident plans that have been wrecked through the stubborn intractability of human nature: the simple fact that human beings have a disquieting and deeply disturbing tendency to say "Yes, if we all behaved like that, the world would be a better place"—only to go and do something totally different.

It would be quite unrealistic to expect social intellectual visionaries to be diverted by the contradiction between the way humanity is and always has been, and the way they would like it to be. The great pagan myth of the "Golden Age," when people were rational and unselfish, is ultimately an expression of weariness with people as they are now. We must not allow the rhetoric of great social visionaries to distract us from the dreadful gulf fixed between rhetoric and reality. The doctrine of justification by faith sounds a note of somber realism, places a question mark against the confident declarations of the vision aries, and raises doubts about the fundamental perfectability (or even reformability!) of human nature. It is, however, a critical, not a negative, approach to ethics, whether personal or social. It warns us of the false prophets of naive moral optimism, insisting that human nature in its totality—from the highest to the lowest of human faculties—is permeated by sin. Even those who are reluctant to call this inborn and inbuilt discord "sin" are prepared to recognize its reality—witness the famous words of the atheist poet A. E. Housman:

The troubles of our proud and angry dust
Are from eternity, and shall not fail.

This insight, however, does not of necessity lead to some form of cynical pessimism, as some ethical writers appear to suggest. The Reformers stressed that—viewed from the *theological*, but not the *ethical*, standpoint—human virtue and morality are "like filthy rags" (Isa. 64:6). In the face of the moral optimism of much Renaissance thought, the Reformers insisted that there is a flaw in human nature that prevents people from achieving their true destiny and renders them impotent to come unaided to that saving knowledge of God for which they are created. They asserted that man, considered from the ethical standpoint, is a mixture of good and evil. (Luther's famous phrase *simul iustus et peccator*, "at one and the same time both righteous and a sinner," is often cited in this connection.) But only a third-rate student of the Reformation would suggest that the Reformers had no interest in ethics, law, or morality! The writings of the Reformers abound with such concerns! But these concerns are always informed by the insight that human ethical actions cannot redeem the fallen human situation; that even the highest human virtue is tainted and compromised by sin; that even the purest ideals and most disinterested actions of individuals and societies are stained by self-interest and pride.

The doctrine of justification by faith results in a realist approach to Christian ethics, which recognizes that the pursuit of self-interest is an inevitability because of the total permeation of human nature by original sin. The liberal vision of the elimination of such self-centeredness and self-interest by education remains an illusion: education may broaden an individual's horizons, but it still keeps that individual at the center of the panorama. How often have we been reminded that the center of "sin" is "I"? Reinhold Niebuhr—perhaps the most distinguished recent exponent of "Christian realism" in ethics— argues that "where there is history at all, there is freedom; and where there is freedom, there is sin."[6] Original sin finds its ethical expression in ineradicable human self-interest—and any ethical system that overlooks or denies this fact threatens to degenerate into utopian idealism, losing any point of contact with the real human situation. It will, however, be clear that the assertion of the universality of sin does not eradicate moral distinctions within human existence. If sin itself is an inevitability, the actual extent of that sin is open to control.

Although it is often suggested that human social problems are a consequence of human *society*, rather than of human *nature*, the realist approach to ethics suggests that the fallenness of human nature infects the society in which we live. Individual self-interest becomes the corporate egoism of contending groups. These insights suggest that a "perfect society" is impossible in history, simply because of the individuals who compose such a society. Thus the goal of Christian social moral action is not the *perfection* of society but its *amelioration*—to make society better in the realization that it cannot be perfect because of human fallenness. If such insights are right, Christians who wish to be involved in politics and social action must realize that they, like everyone else, must operate within the context of the fallen system of human groups.

It is insights such as these that underlie Martin Luther's famous statement, "Be a sinner and sin boldly—but even more strongly have faith and rejoice in Jesus Christ." In other words, the world is fallen, and if the Christian acts within it, he will sin—but he must act *in faith* that he is doing what is best in the situation, under God's guidance, and rejoice that his sin may be forgiven. To put it crudely, but accurately: the world is fallen, and anyone who acts within it will get his hands dirty—but the only other option available is to retreat from that world altogether. Luther's doctrine of justification governs his thinking on social action: *given* that society is sinful because of human sin, the Christian has a right and a duty to try to make bad things better, recognizing that by becoming involved in this fallen world he cannot avoid being associated with its sin. He must act *in faith*, trusting that his assessment of the situation is as realistic as can be hoped for. And if this seems like blundering around in the darkness, it must be remembered that the human apprehension of ethical situations is notoriously inaccurate. Peter Berger speaks persuasively of the "ethics of ignorance": we are unable to assess complex moral situations accurately, and even less able to make sure that the consequences of our acts are what we expect them to be.

On the basis of this discussion it will be clear that we are placed under obligation to God through our redemptive encounter with him in the act of justification. But what form should that obligation take? There is a real danger that talk about our obligation towards the living God will remain abstract and formal unless we are able to ground it in the concrete realities of human existence. It remains an idea, whereas what is required is action. It will be obvious that a discussion of the *nature* of such action must lie far beyond the scope of this work: what we have been primarily concerned with is establishing the foundation upon which any responsible Christian ethics must be based. The doctrine of justification forces us to adopt a critical, but not a negative, attitude towards ethical systems. We learn to ask whether an ethical system is capable of coping with both the transformation of the situation of the moral agent and the sheer intractability of human sinfulness. The doctrine of justification does not stipulate any specific ethical system—it establishes the framework by which such ethical systems are to be judged.

Earlier we noted that the ethical concept of the "imitation of Christ" must be treated cautiously and critically. All too often, the concept is based on serious deficiencies in both Christology (Christ is treated simply as an example) and soteriology (the actions of the Christian believer are regarded as causing, or contributing to, his salvation, rather than expressing what has already been accomplished in Christ). Nevertheless, the concept of the "imitation of Christ" may be allowed a positive role in Christian ethics as long as these deficiencies are avoided. The "shape" of the life of Christ maps out the shape of the believer's life, in that the believer's existence is understood to be broadly patterned after that of Jesus Christ. But, in the end, the doctrine of justification reminds us that the very existence of that believing life constitutes the supreme significance of Jesus Christ for Christian ethics.

FOR FURTHER READING

James Gustafson. *Theology and Ethics*. Chicago: University of Chicago Press, 1981.

Oliver O'Donovan. *Resurrection and Moral Order: An Outline for Evangelical Ethics*. Grand Rapids: Eerdmans, 1986.

Paul Ramsey. *Basic Christian Ethics*. New York: Scribner, 1950.

————. *Deeds and Rules in Christian Ethics*. New York: Scribner, 1967.

Helmut Thielicke. *Theological Ethics*. 3 vols. Grand Rapids: Eerdmans, 1978.

John B. Webster. "Christology, Imitability and Ethics." *Scottish Journal of Theology* 39/3 (1986): 309–26.

9 CONCLUSION

We conclude by summarizing the importance and relevance of this doctrine under five headings.

1. Justification by Faith Concerns an Experience

Underlying the Christian faith is first and foremost an experience, rather than the acceptance of a set of doctrines. The New Testament bears powerful witness to the experience of the first Christians—an experience of the presence and power of the risen Christ in their lives, charging them with meaning and dignity. The experience of being crucified, having died to the world, and being caught up in the life of the risen Christ runs through the fabric of the New Testament as its golden thread. Christ was experienced and known as the risen Lord. This strongly experiential aspect of Christianity tends to be played down by academics, who understandably wish to concentrate on the intellectual framework of the faith—but this must not allow us to overlook the importance of religious experience in the Christian life.

The essential purpose of Christian doctrine is to provide a framework within which the experience of the first Christians may become ours. Just as engineers may construct a channel to bring water from a reservoir to a parched and arid desert area in order that it might flourish and blossom, so Christian doctrine provides the intellectual framework by which the experience of the first Christians may be passed down to us. It must never be forgotten that the great patristic debates about the incarnation and the Trinity were not undertaken for want of something

129

better to do in the long hot Syrian afternoons! It was felt, and felt rightly, that certain doctrines of God and Christ—in other words, certain intellectual frameworks—were inadequate to convey the Christian experience of redemption in Christ. There was a contradiction between the intellectual framework and experience. Let us illustrate this briefly before passing on to the main point.

In the case of Arianism, an important fourth-century Christo-logical heresy, the intellectual framework made it impossible to allow that the Christian experience, mediated through the risen Christ, was of *God*. Arius' views on the identity of Jesus—whom he treated as a quasi-divine figure, but *not* as God—made it impossible for doctrine and experience to be held together. The two would have drifted apart. As Thomas Carlyle observed, "If the Arians had won, Christianity would have dwindled to a legend." Nazareth and Calvary would have no greater significance for us than Long Island or Tower Hill. It was the recognition of the need to ensure that the intellectual framework and the experience it mediated were consistent with each other that forced the clarification of doctrines upon the church. Just as a channel has to be dredged in order to allow the current to flow, so the intellectual framework had to be overhauled to ensure that the Christian experience of God in Christ could be mediated through it.

The importance of the doctrine of justification by faith relates to precisely this point. This doctrine constitutes the intellectual framework by which the Christian experience is transmitted from one generation to another. It creates the expectation that an encounter with God *is* possible and indicates how obstacles to this experience (such as self-righteousness) may be removed. It is the channel through which the Christian experience is passed down. The Reformation period in particular represents an instance of the recognition of the need to dredge this channel, to remove obstacles to this experience. The doctrine affirms that that which so excited and moved the first Chris-tians—the experience of the risen and redeeming Christ—is available today, and it lays the foundation for the appropriation of this experience.

Our interest in the doctrine concerns what it points to, what it *makes available*—a reality that is sometimes obscured by the unfamiliarity of the technical term "justification by faith" both to lay people and to those outside the Christian church. Many technical terms are unfamiliar and seem to be irrelevant to everyday life—and yet they describe something that is actually vital to our way of life. This is as true in law as it is in theology. The "Fifth Amendment to the Constitution" is a technical term that refers to a fundamental principle of American democracy. Even if the term is unfamiliar, the ideas it expresses are not. The same point can be made about many medical terms, hopelessly technical in themselves, which nevertheless refer to fundamental aspects of the way in which the human body works—to realities upon which our lives may ultimately rest. The important point—whether in law, medicine, or theology—is to *explain* the reality that underlies the terminology. And it is the task of the Christian preacher and teacher to *explain* just what the doctrine of "justification by faith" means to us as human beings in the sight of God.

2. Justification by Faith Concerns a Paradox

Any attempt to speak about God involves paradox for the simple reason that God cannot be comprehended in human words or, indeed, in any categories of our finite thought. Our experience of God—who he is, and how he is present and active in the world—cannot be reduced to simple logical statements. To try to do this is to treat God as if he were an "It" rather than a "You" (using Martin Buber's terms; see pp. 98–104). We cannot study God as if he were an object—if we did, theology would certainly make far more sense, but the price paid for this enhanced intelligibility would be a total loss of the *real* God and the substitution of an *idea of God* we felt we could handle! The difficulty lies simply in *expressing in words* what we *experience.* As we emphasized a moment ago, Christianity is primarily about an experience of God through Christ—and when we try to state that experience in words, we find ourselves groping about for ways of trying to express something that is virtually inexpressible.

The doctrine of justification by faith is an excellent example of the inevitability of paradox in conceptualizing, or putting into human language, an experience. The paradox concerns the relationship between ourselves and God in our justification. Christian experience points to the conclusion that every good thing about us, every good thing we do, is somehow not done by us, but is done by God. This is particularly well expressed by Paul, who captures this paradox perfectly. "By the grace of God I am what I am, and his grace to me was not without effect. No, I worked harder than all of them—yet not I, but the grace of God that was with me" (1 Cor. 15:10). On the one hand it was unquestionably Paul who was working hard—but Paul interpreted his experience in terms of God being at work within him. We remain morally responsible and free individuals—and yet we recognize that, somehow, our very freedom is grounded in something God did first.

We noted this paradox in the case of Augustine's controversy with Pelagius (p. 38). Although it is, according to Augustine, the believer who responds to God at conversion, the believer recognizes that God has prepared the way for that conversion and even has taken the upper hand *in* that conversion. Yet the individual makes the choice freely. It is not as if one part of the process could be ascribed to God and the other to the human agent—rather, God's grace evokes the response of faith, and even in that human response the hand of God must be seen. In fact, the only thing we could really be said to contribute to our justification is the sin God so graciously forgives.

It is this same paradox that underlies the conversion of those who, like Saul of Tarsus, seem to be permanently opposed to the gospel and far removed from God. The story of the conversion of Augustine is yet another instance of the importance of the doctrine of justification by faith—the astonishing fact that God will confront those who are hostile to him and far removed from him, in order to bring them home to himself. As Paul himself knew, reconciliation to God is a possibility held out even to those who seem to have permanently turned their back on God. Perhaps one of the most famous instances of this principle in action is the conversion of the slave-trader John Newton (1725–1807). Aware that he was trapped in his own sinful situation and unable to extricate himself, Newton was overwhelmed by the fact that God still met him in Jesus Christ and brought him home. His famous autobiographical opening lines from *Faith's Review and Expectation* make his awareness of "grace abounding unto the chief of sinners" exceptionally clear:

Amazing grace! (how sweet the sound!)
    That saved a wretch like me;
I once was lost, but now am found;
    Was blind, but now I see.

In practice, many evangelistic preachers find it difficult to cope with this paradox. When they are praying, they will gladly ask God to convert their hearers (working on the assumption that it is God who does the converting). When they are preaching, they will give their hearers the impression that it is *they* who have the choice to respond to God (working on the assumption that it is a free human response). It is this situation that has given rise to the famous jibe that they are "Calvinists on their knees, and Arminians in the pulpit."

Why is this paradox, so characteristic a feature of the doctrine of justification, so important? Simply stated, it is important because it deliberately excludes two inadequate understandings of the way in which God and human beings interact in justification: On the one hand the view that we are mere puppets in the hands of the Almighty, who are coerced into salvation whether we like it or not (the universalist position); on the other hand the view that it is we, and we alone, who decide whether or not to respond to God. In this latter case, "election" means that we choose God, rather than the other way round. The paradox of grace—which is ultimately safeguarded by the doctrine of predestination—affirms that it is just not this simple. In some way, God is involved in our justification, even in the response we make to his offer of grace. It is best to see this paradox as a safety check against dangerous simplifications of the gospel, particularly against those that present the gospel as an option that we are totally autonomous in accepting or rejecting. While there is a human side to every action, the Christian gains the impression—an impression that is difficult to put into words—that there is a divine side as well, and that this divine side is actually prior to the human side. For Augustine, this was the mystery of prevenient grace—grace that "goes before" us, preparing the way for us. It cannot be explained—but it must be recognized if we are to remain faithful to the Christian understanding of the way in which God is at work in his world.

3. Justification by Faith Concerns Personal Humility

The doctrine of justification by faith affirms that we are what we are by grace through faith—God gives, and we receive. The gospel portrayal of the believer's childlike trust in God, his Father, perfectly captures the attitude towards God which the doctrine of justification by faith suggests. As Calvin pointed out, we come to God with empty open hands, knowing that we have nothing to give and everything to receive. It is to God that we pray for the gifts he gives, knowing that we are ultimately dependent on God for our spiritual existence and development. We are totally dependent on God—a dependence we must recognize and incorporate into our understanding of ourselves and our relation to God. Whereas the Pelagian theologian Julian of Eclanum declared that we are "emancipated from God" and are free to live in our own strength and freedom, the doctrine of justification by faith affirms that we are weak and frail, requiring God's support and grace throughout our existence.

Augustine of Hippo likened the Christian church to a hospital full of people who are ill and have recognized the need for the assistance of a physician if they are to recover. The doctrine of justification by faith diagnoses our spiritual illness (sin) and offers us an effective cure (grace), made available through the death and resurrection of Jesus Christ. We are offered that cure, but must receive it if it is to heal us. Thus Augustine interprets the parable of the good Samaritan (Luke 10:25–37) as illustrating the compassion of Jesus Christ for sinful humanity. We are wounded and left half-dead through sin, and Christ the physician comes to our aid to make us whole. The two silver coins (Luke 10:35) represent the sacraments of baptism and the eucharist, by which God gives us grace. When we receive communion, we usually kneel with empty open hands to receive the bread, just as we come before God himself with empty open hands, with nothing to offer or give except ourselves, and everything to receive from a gracious God. It is this attitude of dependence on God that the doctrine of justification affirms as essential to an authentically Christian existence. In the words of Augustus Toplady,

> Nothing in my hand I bring,
> Simply to thy Cross I cling;
> Naked come to thee for dress,
> Helpless, look to thee for grace;
> Foul, I to the fountain fly,
> Wash me, Savior, or I die.

4. *Justification by Faith Concerns an Overturning of Secular Values*

The doctrine of justification establishes and upholds a central insight that both the Old and New Testaments proclaim with force: that God chooses those who are weak or foolish in the eyes of the world—indeed, even in their own eyes!—in order to work through them. "Brothers, think of what you were when you were called. Not many of you were wise by human standards; not many were influential; not many were of noble birth. But God chose the foolish things of the world to shame the wise; God chose the weak things of the world to shame the strong" (1 Cor. 1:26–28). It is not what they *are* that matters—it is what they are prepared to allow God to *do through them*. Let us illustrate this point to bring out its full importance.

The Old Testament frequently draws attention to the fact that the great men of faith were not called by God on account of their status, position, or wealth. Thus God called Abraham, not because he *was* great, but in order to *make* him great (Gen. 12:1–3). God did not choose Israel because she was powerful or mighty, but because he loved her (Deut. 7:7–10). Similarly, God chose Gideon to deliver Israel from the Midianites, despite the fact that Gideon's position within Israel was insignificant. As Gideon himself protested, "How can I save Israel? My clan is the weakest in Manasseh, and I am the least in my family" (Judg. 6:15). And yet, once more, the pattern is set: God chooses the weak, the lowly, the humble, and the insignificant in order to make them great. Perhaps the most striking—and certainly the most famous!—illustration of this principle is to be found in the story of Samuel's search for the Lord's anointed one (1 Sam. 16:1–13). Knowing that one of Jesse's sons is to be anointed king of Israel, Samuel assumes that Eliab has been chosen, because of his obvious great stature. But the word of the Lord comes to him, "Do not consider his appearance or his height, for I have rejected him. The Lord does not look at the things man looks at. Man looks at the outward appearance, but the Lord looks at the heart" (v. 7). And so Samuel eventually recognizes the youngest son, David, who has been sent off to look after the sheep, as the Lord's anointed one. And as the story of David and Goliath makes clear (ch. 17), David is able to conquer in weakness where others were defeated in their strength, because he trusted in the Lord.

The same principle is developed in the New Testament, especially by Paul. Paul himself was acutely aware that in choosing him as an apostle, God has picked someone who was totally unworthy of this high office. In the eyes of the world, Paul was virtually excluded from becoming an apostle. However, God was able to take this unpromising material, and make of it what he wanted. "For I am the least of the apostles, and do not even deserve to be called an apostle, because I persecuted the church of God. But by the grace of God I am what I am" (1 Cor. 15:9–10). It is this theme which Paul expounds with some force in his "theology of the cross" (1 Cor. 1:18–2:5), in which the great theme of God's choosing what the world regards as weak and foolish is developed with considerable skill. God takes those who know that they are nothing, in order to make them into something which they otherwise could not be. God chooses the humble, in order to elevate them (Luke 2:52; 18:9–14). The great theme here developed is that of God taking something small, in order to make it into something great and significant in his eyes which he may use to good effect in his plans for the world—and it is this theme that is grounded in and expounded by the doctrine of justification by faith.[1]

5. Justification by Faith Concerns the Future of Christianity

How will Christianity survive in the future? In the past, the Christian church in Europe and North America alike has relied too much on a favorable cultural milieu for its survival, knowing that its existence was safeguarded by social patterns of behavior. While this state of affairs continued, the doctrine of justification by faith was neglected, because it was seen as lacking relevance and urgency. But this state of affairs may not continue. How will the Christian faith and the Christian church survive if social factors favoring church membership are reversed?

It is here that the doctrine of justification by faith assumes its specific and peculiar importance. The doctrine underlies all evangelism, the proclamation of Christ to the world. As we have seen, the doctrine affirms that the same experience that stamped its powerful impression upon the New Testament is available today, here and now. It affirms that individuals may here and now be caught up in the Christian experience of the risen Christ. It exults in the sheer *attractiveness* of Christianity, motivating individuals to *want* to become Christians. In a day and age when belief must be won, rather than assumed, the doctrine of justification fulfills a crucial role. It is the *articulus stantis et cadentis ecclesiae*, the "article by which the church stands or falls." The Christian church takes its stand against a disbelieving world on the basis of the firm and constant belief that God *acted* in the death and resurrection of Jesus Christ to achieve something that will remain of permanent significance to human beings, so long as they walk the face of this planet knowing that they must die. We are exposed for what we really are—sinners—and are offered the possibility of transformation as a free gift of God. The life of the Christian church—its doctrine, worship, and proclamation—is based on the knowledge that God has established a new relationship between himself and sinful humanity through the death and resurrection of Jesus Christ, and that this relationship constitutes the only basis for authentic human existence on the face of this earth. The great themes of authenticity, of forgiveness, of eternal life, of meaningfulness, of purpose—all these are affirmed and expounded by the doctrine of justification by faith. This is the spiritual heritage that has been passed down from one generation of believers to another, like the torch of liberty, and we must pass it on to those who follow. For the gospel of the gracious justification of sinful humanity by a living and loving God is the pearl of great price of which we are the temporary stewards, and we must safeguard, defend, and *use* this vital doctrine on their behalf. A generation is waiting to be born, to discover the graciousness of the living God, and to respond to it—and we, like the runners in a relay race, must be poised and ready to hand over to them what has been entrusted to us for a time—the doctrine of justification by faith.

APPENDIX:
THE DOGMATIC SIGNIFICANCE
OF THE DOCTRINE

At the center of the Christian faith stands the person of Jesus Christ. To each and every generation, the same fundamental question is addressed: "Who do *you* say that I am?" (Matt. 16:15). The answers which the Christian faith proclaims to the fundamental and central questions of life—who God is, and what he is like; our own nature and destiny—all center upon the figure of Jesus Christ. Who is this remarkable figure? And why is he judged to be so important? The question of who Jesus *is* cannot, however, be divorced from the question of what Jesus *does for us*.[1] Jesus' identity and function—who he is and what he does—are simply the two sides of the same coin. Perhaps the most famous statement of this general principle comes from the German Reformer Philip Melanchthon: "This is to know Christ: to know his benefits." Who Jesus Christ is becomes known through his saving action—and Jesus Christ's saving action is only possible in the first place because of who he is. Thus our interest in the person of Jesus Christ is primarily motivated by our interest in the salvation that is proclaimed in his name. The growing agreement among theologians that Christology (the question of the *identity* of Jesus Christ) cannot be considered in isolation from soteriology (the question of what Jesus Christ *does for us*) has led to a growing interest in and concern for the latter.[2]

The assumption that reconciliation to God through Jesus Christ is a present reality for those inside the church and a present possibility for those outside it underlies the Christian proclamation of the gospel. To proclaim Christ is to proclaim his benefits. The essence of the Christian proclamation is that, sinners though we are (and sinners though we will remain!), we really may be reconciled to the living God through the death and resurrection of Jesus Christ. How can this be so? we naturally ask. We find it difficult to accept that we have been accepted, despite being unacceptable. How can it be that the holy and righteous God should enter into a relationship with sinners like us? Theories about how this might be possible are, however, secondary to the simple fact that it *is* possible! It is through the proclamation of this astonishing fact that the church takes her stand against a disbelieving world. The Christian church proclaims the possibility of transforming the human situation, of resolving the human dilemma, through confrontation with the crucified and risen Christ.

The central feature of the Christian proclamation is that God offers us salvation *as a gift* through the death and resurrection of Jesus Christ. Moral or religious renewal is not a precondition of forgiveness—forgiveness is offered to us unconditionally, as a gift of God. We come to God empty-handed, having nothing to offer except that which we receive by the grace of God. That gift, however, brings with it our transformation. Just as the planting of the seed leads to the bearing of fruit, so forgiveness leads to renewal and regeneration. To invert this order, and to suggest that forgiveness is conditional, depending upon renewal and regeneration, is to abandon a crucial insight of the gospel and to degenerate into some form of moralism, such as that associated with the Enlightenment of the eighteenth century. The gift of God precedes his demands and brings with it renewal and transformation.

Having recognized that something remarkable and astonishing, of permanent relevance to the human situation, was achieved by God through the death and resurrection of Jesus Christ, the first Christians were obliged to try and put this into words. This proved difficult: how could the richness and vitality of their experience of a redeeming encounter with the living God ever be expressed in mere words? The New Testament documents, particularly the letters of Paul, show how various ideas were used to try to express what had been accomplished through the death and resurrection of Jesus Christ. Redemption, salvation, forgiveness, justification, reconciliation[3]—all these ideas illuminated one or more aspects of the greater reality of what God has done for us in Jesus Christ.

Although none of these ideas was adequate in itself to describe exhaustively what the "benefits of Christ" are, they combined to build up an overall picture of what is involved. Just as the individual pieces of a jigsaw, or an artist's individual brush-strokes, build up to reveal a picture, so these ideas combined to reveal the overall shape of the experience of the first Christians when they encountered the living God through the crucified and risen Christ. And their experience has become our experience—just as their difficulties in adequately describing it have become our difficulties!

As theologians wrestled with the richness of the biblical conception of God's redeeming action in the cross and resurrection of Jesus Christ, one idea began to emerge as the most convenient summary of the nature and purpose of that action— "justification by faith."[4] This leading idea of the gospel, particularly as expressed in the letters of Paul (see, for example, Rom. 5:1), came to be seen as encapsulating the essence of the New Testament proclamation: We are offered forgiveness, redemption, and salvation as a gift through the death and resurrection of Jesus Christ and are transformed through this creative encounter with the living God. As we indicated in the first part of this work, this central insight has constantly come under threat during the history of the Christian church. It is for this reason that the doctrine of justification by faith has often assumed a polemical, or controversial, role—challenging inadequate or inaccurate understandings of how we are reconciled to the living God.

In fact, the doctrine of justification by faith has now come to have a meaning that is virtually independent of its Pauline origins. In systematic theology, the doctrine of justification by faith has come to refer to the gracious restoration of man's broken relationship with God through the crucifixion and resurrection of Jesus Christ. It is this assumption that underlies the proclamation of the church—the fact that a real, genuine, and authentic personal relationship with the living God is possible, here and now. It is on the basis of this firm and certain belief that the church of God takes its stand against a disbelieving world. The doctrine of justification by faith proclaims the possibility of a total alteration of the human situation through accepting this gift. It declares that peace may be

concluded between a holy and righteous God and sinful
humanity. It asserts that a transition is possible between a dead
and godless human existence and the living and vital relationship with the God and Father of our Lord Jesus Christ. The
church of God stands or falls with the truth of this assertion—
and it is for this reason that the doctrine of justification is often
designated "the article by which the church stands or falls
(*articulus stantis et cadentis ecclesiae*)."[5]

It is clear that both the Old and the New Testament regard
justification as a transformational experience—in other words,
justification changes us, initiating a new relationship with God
that is charged with a creative power to transform us. As we
saw in earlier chapters, Christian theology has expressed this
important insight in a number of ways. For Augustine,
justification included both the *event* of being *declared* to be
righteous and the *process* of being *made* righteous. For Calvin,
two aspects of this one entity could be distinguished—the *event*
of *justification* (in which we are declared to be righteous) and the
process of *regeneration or sanctification*, in which we are made
righteous. As Calvin emphasizes, justification and sanctification are to be regarded as two aspects of the same divine
act (1 Cor. 6:11)—indeed, Calvin refers to them together as
"the double grace." It will, of course, be obvious that Augustine and Calvin use the term "justification" to mean different
things (Augustine meaning by "justification" what Calvin
means by "justification" and "sanctification" together). Obviously, this has given rise to considerable confusion, as we saw
(pp. 56–61). It is a matter for debate which of these two
positions is more faithful to the biblical witness—but in each
case, the basic idea remains the same: something happens that
initiates a creative encounter with the risen Christ, an encounter through which we are both forgiven and renewed. God
meets us where we are, but he doesn't just leave us there! The
offer of pardon and forgiveness carries with it the promise of
transformation and renewal. When God promises the removal
of our condemnation, thus giving us a new status before him,
he also begins to refashion us and renew us through grace.
Underlying all these related themes is the basic content of the
doctrine of justification by faith: that God offers himself to us in
Jesus Christ, and that the resulting union with Jesus Christ

through faith brings about our inner renewal and transformation. The gift that God offers to us in justification is nothing other than himself. In justification, God offers to dwell within us as his temple and do for us what we could never hope to achieve for ourselves. It is this idea that underlies the most difficult verse of John Henry Newman's famous hymn "Praise to the Holiest in the Height":

And that a higher gift than grace
Should flesh and blood refine
God's presence and his very self
And essence all-divine.

It is helpful to make a distinction at this point between the *concept of justification* and the *doctrine of justification*. The concept of justification is one of several such concepts used by the New Testament (and especially Paul) to build up a comprehensive picture of what the "benefits of Christ" involve. The concept of justification speaks to us of the removal of condemnation and the establishment of a new relationship and status with God (Rom. 3:22–27; 4:5; 5:1–5). The idea of adoption points to our new identity as children of God (Rom. 8:15–17). The concepts of reconciliation and forgiveness point to the restoration of broken relationships (2 Cor. 5:18–21; Eph. 2:13–18). The concepts of redemption and liberation point to rescue from bondage and slavery, and the price paid by God in Christ for this (Mark 10:45; Eph. 1:7). Here, justification is an important, but not exhaustive, description of what the "shape" of our new life in Jesus Christ is like.

The *doctrine* of justification, however, is concerned with the fundamental question of how the "benefits of Christ" may be appropriated. How may this new life in Jesus Christ be begun? What must the individual *do* if he is to meet God in Christ in this transforming encounter? The doctrine of justification is the thin end of the wedge of Christian theology in that it is this doctrine that confronts an individual with the means by which he may enter the community of faith. It is this doctrine that controls the gateway to the church. It is this doctrine that controls the Christian preaching of Jesus Christ. Even if it could be shown that the *concept* of justification is not central to Christian theology, this would not allow us to draw the conclusion that the *doctrine* of justification lacks this centrality. In a day and age when the Christian church has to win the hearts and minds of men and women, rather than rely upon a favorable cultural milieu for church membership, the doctrine of justification assumes a new importance—because it is concerned with the winning of men and women for Christ by setting before them what Christ has done for them and how they may make this their own.

The doctrine of justification by faith has thus, for both theological and historical reasons, come to designate the astonishing affirmation that God meets us where we are through Jesus Christ, embraces us, and takes us home. It affirms both human sinfulness and the graciousness of God. Without sin, there is no need for justification—and without grace, there is no possibility of justification. The doctrine of justification by faith asserts that the real personal and transforming presence of Christ within believers is given as a gift. It is conceivable that this emphasis upon justification goes beyond the New Testament statements on the matter. But even if this is the case, it does not affect the importance of the doctrine. "Justification by faith" is best regarded as a slogan, a cipher, a shorthand way of affirming a crucial insight of the Christian faith: that we come to God empty-handed and broken, to receive a gift which far exceeds anything we can imagine and anything we deserve—the real and redeeming presence of the crucified and risen Christ within us, and the promise of forgiveness, renewal, and eternal life.

A similar situation has arisen within English-language theology in relation to the word "atonement," and it will be instructive to compare the two cases. The term "atonement" has come to be treated as equivalent to "the work of Jesus Christ." If you pick up one of the many books with the phrase "the atonement" in its title, you can be sure that its subject matter is what Christ achieved through his death upon the cross. The origins of this development are historical. In the early sixteenth century, the English Reformer William Tyndale translated the New Testament into English. Tyndale translated the Greek word *katallage* (now generally translated as "reconciliation") as "atonement." It is obvious that Tyndale took "at-one-ment" to mean what we understand by "reconciliation." The term "atonement," however, rapidly acquired a developed meaning—"the grounds on which reconciliation to God is possible." And just as one of St. Paul's soteriological terms has come to mean "the grounds on which reconciliation to God is possible," so another (justification) has come to mean "the free gift of salvation in Jesus Christ."

At this point it may be helpful to distinguish two related areas of Christian doctrine that are often confused. It is necessary to draw a careful distinction between the following:

1. *The grounds of justification.* This deals with the question how justification is actually *possible* in the first place. Why can a holy and righteous God enter into fellowship with a sinner? With this question, we are asking about the objective basis of our justification, the grounds upon which it is ultimately possible. This question is dealt with by the area of theology often referred to as either "the doctrine of the work of Christ" or "the doctrine of the Atonement."

2. *The doctrine of justification.* This *assumes* the objective grounds of justification—in other words, that it really is possible for God to justify sinners—and moves on to ask a more pressing and practical question: What must we do if we are to make this relationship a reality? How do we actualize this exciting possibility?

We could say that the doctrine of the atonement, or of the work of Christ, deals with the question *why justification is possible,* and the doctrine of justification with the question *what must be done if we are to be justified.* The former is a little theoretical, but the latter is very practical and of enormous importance to Christian preaching, counseling, and evangelism. An analogy may bring this point out.

Let us suppose that you are in your automobile in a parking lot and want to get across town to an important meeting. You need to get the motor started. What do you do? You insert the key in the ignition, and turn it—and the motor turns over and starts. Why does this happen? Well, turning the key completes an electrical circuit, which energizes a motor, which turns the engine over, while at the same time generating a high tension discharge at the spark plugs, which ignites the gasoline, causing controlled explosions, which force the pistons down. . . . And so on. We are dealing with two questions, one very practical one (what do I do to get going?) and one much more theoretical (how come that all this happens when I do that?). The doctrine of justification is basically about what you need to do to get going in the Christian faith, while the doctrine of Christ is about why this is possible in the first place. And, to take this analogy just a little further, the work of Christ is what powers our justification, just like the motor powers the automobile.

Another way of illuminating the relationship between the doctrines of the atonement and of justification is the following. Imagine an enormous hydroelectric plant, with thousands of tons of water pouring down every second to be turned into electrical power—or a coal or oil-fired furnace generating an enormous amount of heat to drive the great turbines powering the generators. You can sense the power, the energy of these plants, through the roar of the machinery and whine of the generators. Now imagine you're in a workshop, with an electrically powered lathe. You throw a switch, and the lathe comes to life—the electric motor builds up speed and momentum, ready for action. The power of that vast amount of water, the energy of those great furnaces, is now available for your use. In many ways, this illustrates the relationship between atonement and justification. Atonement is the powerhouse of the Christian faith, the source of the new life of the Christian and the basis on which the power of God becomes ours. But we still have to make the connection by appropriating that power, by switching in to it. And justification is rather like throwing a switch: It is through justification that the "benefits of Christ" become ours, are actualized in our lives. They are both essential links in the same chain—one deals with the "why," the other with the "how."

The Christian faith itself stands or falls with the fundamental declaration that God has in Christ established a new relationship between himself and sinners, and the life of faith stands or falls with the knowledge of this decisive action on the part of God. If this belief is false, the Christian faith must be recognized as a delusion—a deeply satisfying delusion, to be sure, but a delusion none the less. But if it is true, it is of central and decisive importance to the Christian understanding of the meaning of life, human nature and destiny, and the nature and purposes of God. The doctrine of justification by faith touches human existence at its heart, at the point of its relation to God. It defines the preaching of the Christian church, the establishment and development of the life of faith, the basis of human security and our perspective for the future. So important was the doctrine for Martin Luther that he stated it to be "the master and ruler, lord, governor and judge over all other doctrines, which preserves and governs every Christian doctrine and upholds our conscience before God." Once grasped, the importance of the doctrine for every aspect of Christian life—theology, spirituality, and ethics—must be explored and acted on.

Like many college students, I once had to study mathematics. One of the areas of that subject which I found particularly interesting was vectors. A vector is basically a force acting in a certain direction, and one of the problems we were usually asked to solve was to work out its relative strength in other directions. This was referred to as "resolving a vector into its components" along the three-dimensional axes x, y, and z. And just as a vector V may be transformed around the x, y, and z axes to give the components V_x, V_y, and V_z, so the doctrine of justification requires transformation about the theological, spiritual, and ethical axes in order to allow its theological, spiritual, and ethical components to be identified. We must ask what the implications are of the remarkable assertion that God offers us our salvation as a gift through the death and resurrection of Jesus Christ.

The doctrine of justification by faith contains within itself the germs of the leading doctrines of the Christian faith. It contains certain concepts of God, Christ, and human nature which assume a specifically *Christian* meaning when properly interpreted. By declaring that this doctrine stands at the center of the Christian faith, we are actually defining both the real center and the actual limits of its theological system. This has four important results:

1. The saving action of God in the death and resurrection of Jesus Christ is declared to be at the center and heart of the Christian faith.
2. Any necessary presuppositions or consequences of this doctrine must be regarded as essential to the Christian faith.
3. Any opinions that are necessarily excluded by the doctrine must be regarded as non-Christian or anti-Christian, allowing a provisional definition of the limits of the Christian faith.
4. Any matters on which the doctrine has no direct bearing must be regarded either as *adiaphora*, "matters of indifference," or else as matters that may be resolved by the application of other, secondary, criteria.

We shall consider the first three of these points individually.

1. By affirming that God's saving action in Jesus Christ lies at the heart of the Christian faith, we are suggesting that responsible theological speculation must begin with, be based upon, and be governed by, that action. It is this action that brought the Christian faith and the Christian church into being, and gives it its grounds for existence. For Martin Luther, this recognition led to the formulation of the "theology of the cross" (*theologia crucis*)—the assertion that theology is not concerned with abstract speculation about metaphysics but with the concrete event of the cross and resurrection of Jesus Christ.[6] It is at this point that the central concerns of the Christian faith converge, just as the spokes that support the rim of a wheel converge upon the central hub.

Martin Luther took this point with full seriousness, making the following statement about the nature of Christian theology: "The proper subject of theology is man as a thing of sin and the justifying God, the savior of sinful man." Luther's statement is of considerable importance in the face of the perennial tendency on the part of much academic theology to see its task in terms of philosophical speculation rather than reflection upon the self-revelation of God in the death and resurrection of Jesus Christ. Theology doesn't set its own agenda—it has its agenda set for it by the Christian proclamation. For Luther, God is to be conceived as the one who justifies sinners, rather than as an abstract concept. Similarly, the idea that we can have "objective knowledge" of God is to be rejected: our knowledge of God is never disinterested but is a response to God's faithfulness to his promises of salvation. God addresses us as the one who justifies us, who calls us to stand within his covenant of grace, who offers us eternal life through the death and resurrection of Jesus Christ. This is no objective historical knowledge of God— it is a creative and redeeming knowledge that promises to transform our existence.

The "truth that sets us free" (John 8:32) is not some form of abstract knowledge—it is Jesus himself (John 8:36), the concrete expression of the saving will and actions of God. It is in Jesus Christ that we have knowledge of ourselves as sinful and God as our redeemer. It is the death and resurrection of Jesus Christ that brought the Christian faith and the Christian church into being, and gives it its grounds for existence. The "theology of the cross" is diametrically opposed to our natural tendency to want to conceptualize God and insists that God is not some idea or concept which we can just play around with in some seminar room, but that he is none other than the living God who acts in our history in order to transform it. God takes the initiative away from us by moving first, by acting to justify and redeem us in Jesus Christ.

A similar point was made by John Calvin. In his famous *Institutes of the Christian Religion*, Calvin pointed out that knowledge of God is of two types—"knowledge of God the creator" (*cognitio Dei creatoris*) and "knowledge of God the redeemer" (*cognitio Dei redemptoris*). The former is open to anyone who bothers to look at the night sky or reflect on the beauty and orderliness of creation. The knowledge of God the redeemer, however, is a specifically Christian form of knowledge and is concentrated in and focused on the crucified and risen Jesus Christ and the witness to him in Holy Scripture. Thus for Calvin the distinctively Christian insight into God concerns the fact that he acted to redeem us in Christ. This is not to deny that he created us in the first place—Christianity shares this belief with Islam, Judaism, and deism. But Christianity comes into its own through the recognition that God

acted to redeem his creation, to re-create it, through Jesus
Christ.

The historical relevance of this point is obvious. The first
Christians had no hesitation in worshipping Jesus Christ as
their Savior and their Lord, and the early patristic christological
and trinitarian debates were primarily concerned with uphold-
ing the fundamental belief that it was only through Jesus Christ
that mankind could be redeemed. Historically, there are
excellent reasons for suggesting that it was the recognition of
the fact that "God was reconciling the world to himself in
Christ" (2 Cor. 5:19) that led to the recognition of the divinity
of Jesus Christ. Even in the Arian controversy of the fourth
century, the conviction that Christ was the sole redeemer of
mankind constituted the common ground between the two
opposing views of Christ.

The importance of this point for a correct understanding of
the nature and task of Christian theology will also be evident.
There has been a tendency in much recent academic theology to
drive a wedge between preaching and theology—yet it is
evident that the two are closely related. Preaching is basically
the re-presentation of the saving act of God in Jesus Christ to
the present generation, an attempt to confront humanity with
the possibility, the actuality, and the necessity of being
reconciled to the living God through the death and resurrection
of Jesus Christ. It is through responding to this call, through
coming to the crucified and risen Christ, that faith is born. The
Christian proclamation is basically the distillation or summary
of the significance of Jesus Christ for the human situation,
linked with an invitation and challenge to make this significance our own. And it is unthinkable that Christian
theology should drive a wedge between what is perhaps the
most important task of the Christian church—the proclamation
of Christ as Savior and Lord to the world—and the church's
reflection upon its nature and identity.

This point was fully appreciated by Karl Barth, who regarded
theology as a critical and positive tool for the undergirding of
the Christian proclamation. Theology is about proclamation—
the preaching of Jesus Christ. And an essential presupposition
of that preaching is that God *has* achieved something through
Jesus Christ. Barth's comments are full of insight:

The Christian community and Christian faith stand or fall
with the reality of the fact that in confirmation of the
covenant broken by man the holy God has set up a new
fellowship between Himself and sinful man, instituting a
new covenant which cannot be destroyed or even dis-
turbed by any transgression on the part of man. The
community rests and acts on this basis. Faith lives by the
certainty and actuality of the reconciliation of the world
with God accomplished in Jesus Christ.[7]

In other words, the Christian church and faith *exist*, and the
Christian proclamation of Jesus Christ *proceeds*, on the basis of
the belief that God has altered the human situation through
Jesus Christ. This is an essential presupposition of Christian
theology and must be recognized as such.[8]

Anselm of Canterbury, the famous eleventh-century arch-
bishop and theologian, defined theology in words that have
gained wide acceptance: theology is "faith seeking understanding" (*fides quaerens intellectum*). In other words, theology is
basically concerned with *understanding* what has already been
believed. And central to that faith—indeed, the *immediate cause*
of that faith—is the recognition of the crucifixion and resurrection of Jesus Christ as the saving act of God. Whatever interests
the theologian may develop, priority is claimed by the need to
explore and explain the consequences of the justification of
sinful humanity for Christian theology (the way we think),
spirituality (the way we pray), and ethics (the way we act). The
gospel brings before us the free gift of God and challenges us to
make this gift the basis of every aspect of our life—and it is the
task of the theologian to work out what bearing our justification
has upon the way in which we think and act. For justification
brings transformation—and part of that transformation is
rethinking every aspect of our existence.

The recognition that the saving action of God in Jesus Christ
stands at the center of the gospel proclamation also allows us to
assign priorities to certain doctrines. An excellent example of
this is provided by the doctrine of predestination. In the New
Testament, this doctrine is overshadowed by the proclamation
of the divine right-making maneuver in the death and resurrection of Jesus Christ. It is seen as part of the substructure of that

maneuver. It is, however, very easy to distort the relative priority the New Testament assigns to the doctrines of predestination and salvation in Christ. To illustrate this point, let us consider the positions of John Calvin and Theodore Beza (a later Reformed theologian) on this matter.[9]

For Calvin, the doctrine of predestination is an aspect of the doctrine of salvation. In the *Institutes*, Calvin does not assign the doctrine of predestination to any particular place of importance—it is one aspect, and certainly not the most important aspect, of our salvation through the death and resurrection of Jesus Christ. Calvin tends to treat the doctrine as a safety check, emphasizing the mysteriousness of divine election, and also cutting the ground from under any suggestion that it is we who choose God. The doctrine of predestination affirms that God has the upper hand in our salvation. Calvin's theological method at this point is *inductive* and *analytic*: he begins with the specific and unique event of the saving death and resurrection of Jesus Christ as the center of his doctrine of salvation, and then sets out from that point to explore its implications. The event is considered first—and only then the theological framework within which it is set. One of those implications is the mystery of predestination and election. But it is the saving event of Jesus Christ himself that is the center of Calvin's thought at this point—not the doctrine of predestination! This point becomes all the more important when the very different approach of Theodore Beza is considered.

For Beza, Christian theology should not begin with the saving event of the death and resurrection of Jesus Christ, but with the theological framework within which this event is set. Beza thus begins with the divine decision to predestine and redeem the elect in Jesus Christ, and then proceeds to deduce the actuality of this redemption of the elect in Christ. Beza thus employs a *synthetic* and *deductive* approach, quite distinct from that of Calvin, which assigns priority to the doctrine of predestination. The logical consistency of Beza's scheme is achieved through replacing the New Testament emphasis upon an *event* with a quite different emphasis (foreign to the New Testament) on a conceptual framework. Furthermore, in keeping with the logical rigor of his theological framework, Beza draws conclusions that are dictated by *logic*, but not by *theology*—for example, that Jesus Christ died only for the elect, a view that is not found in the New Testament itself.

By assigning priority to the doctrine of justification in this way, we are thus able to retain the characteristic New Testament emphasis upon Jesus Christ, upon something that happened in history which is charged with meaning and significance for us. The developments associated with theologians such as Beza take us far away from this concrete event, into the obscure and abstract realms of intra-trinitarian debates. The Christocentricity of the New Testament is preserved and consolidated through the recognition of the priority of the doctrine of justification, in both Christian preaching and theology.

2. As theologians, we are also obliged to consider the presuppositions and consequences of the fact that God has justified us in Jesus Christ. The affirmation that God has acted in this way is like the center of a spider's web—it is supported by a complex structure. It is like the rhododendrons Betty McDonald tried to uproot and transplant on her chicken ranch (what reader of *The Egg and I* can forget that description?)—the little bushes were discovered to have enormous tap roots, not visible from the surface, thrusting deep into the ground. The roots of the Christian proclamation run deep and wide into the rich soil of Christian theology. The part of the Christian proclamation which we encounter—the free justification of humanity through the death and resurrection of Jesus Christ—is supported by a considerable substructure, whose presence is real and vital, even if it is not immediately obvious.

The proclamation of the justification of sinful man through the death and resurrection of Jesus Christ presupposes certain things, and also has certain things as its necessary consequences. As we suggested above, it is necessary to explore these and to recognize them as authentically Christian. We shall illustrate this point with reference to two areas of theology: anthropology (the Christian understanding of human nature) and Christology (the understanding of the identity and significance of Jesus Christ).

For Paul, the "message of the cross" (1 Cor. 1:18) was the

foundation of his mission to Gentiles and Jews alike—the proclamation that everyone, irrespective of their origins or importance, could be reconciled to God through the death and resurrection of Jesus Christ. It will be clear that this extremely positive assertion has a negative presupposition—that everyone, irrespective of their origins or importance, *stands in need of reconciliation to God.* The negative presupposition of justification is therefore sin. Through reflection upon the proclamation of our restoration to fellowship with God through Christ, we are forced to reflect upon the presupposition of this proclamation—that we are alienated from God and require reconciliation to him. The theological understanding of human nature begins with the recognition that we are the object of God's justification.

This point may be developed further. According to Genesis 1:26 we are made in the image of God—and some theologians have suggested that this is an adequate theological understanding of human nature. But as we noted earlier, the characteristically Christian insight into human nature is based upon the knowledge of God as redeemer rather than just as creator. The insight that God created humanity is important, but it is very far from being all that needs to be said about human nature! The doctrine of justification forces us to recognize humanity as a creation of God requiring redemption. The image of God in humanity is real, but tarnished and obscured, and requires renewal and regeneration. The doctrine of justification points not merely to the fact that humanity is created in the image of God but also to the necessity and possibility of the renewal of that divine image by redemption through Christ. It forces us to recognize a tension, a dialectic, between nature and grace. This tension is evident both in individual humans and in human culture. "Because man is God's creature, some of his culture is rich in beauty and goodness. Because he is fallen, all of it is tainted with sin, and some of it is demonic."[10]

It will therefore be clear that one of the presuppositions of the doctrine of justification is a doctrine of original sin. Perhaps the term "original sin" is not particularly helpful in understanding what is involved. The basic idea is that humanity is naturally alienated from God. We enter the world as creatures of God, and are confronted with the possibility of *becoming* children of

God. "Original sin" may be defined as the natural human state, the state in which we are born into the world. It is not a moral concept but refers to the human state with only a nominal relation to God (that of being his creatures), rather than a real relationship (that of being his children). The doctrine of justification affirms that the possibility of that relationship is there. Man is "created in the image of God"—suggesting that there is an inbuilt possibility for exactly that relationship. There is a certain "likeness," a point of contact, between God and us that allows this relationship to be established. Some modern theologians, such as Emil Brunner, have analyzed this in terms of "addressability" (*Ansprechbarkeit*): human beings are capable of being addressed by God and of responding to that gracious address. Although we are born into the world alienated from God, the possibility of being reconciled to God remains open. As the French philosopher Blaise Pascal observed: "There is a God-shaped gap within man." In other words, human nature is unfulfilled until that gap is filled by God—and the doctrine of justification both highlights this deficiency in the natural human state and proclaims the possibility of this situation being radically altered.

The doctrine of justification by faith brings together an important cluster of ideas concerning the *identity and nature* of humanity. It affirms that we are creatures who are elevated above all other creatures by being made in the image of the God who created us and who subsequently addresses us through Jesus Christ. That address discloses to us that we are not what we could and should be, that we are lost and that God has journeyed into the distant country to find us. Our true destiny and fulfillment lie in our restoration to fellowship to God. Justification discloses what we *now are*, what we *are called to be*, and how the transition between these two states may be effected.

As we saw earlier, this point is illuminated by the parable of the prodigal son (Luke 15:11–32). Throughout this story, nothing the son does alters the fact that he is his father's son. But his action in leaving home for the distant country points to this relation existing in name only. He does not act as if he is his father's son. Then, of course, the situation changes: the son returns home to be reconciled to his father and to assume the responsibilities which the relation with his father involves. While he is in the far country, he is his father's son in name only—but on his return, reconciled to his father, that relation ceases to be nominal and becomes real. So it is with God. We enter the world with a *nominal* relation to God—and the possibility of this being converted to a *real* relationship is proclaimed in the gospel.

This does not, of course, mean that the doctrine of original sin has the same importance as the doctrine of redemption through Jesus Christ! We proclaim redemption in Christ as something that is purely positive and exciting, rather than as something that is negative. The doctrine of original sin, like the doctrine of predestination, is part of the theological framework within which the event of the death and resurrection of Jesus Christ is set. It is part of the substructure of the proclamation of the redemption of humanity in Jesus Christ. In affirming the reality and actuality of that redemption we are also affirming a cluster of related, but less important ideas—ideas such as original sin and predestination. The proclamation of redemption is positively good news—but, as we begin to reflect on it, we realize that it has certain negative presuppositions, one of which is that we *need* redemption. And it is this presupposition of our redemption which is expressed in the doctrine of original sin.

Let us take this matter a little farther. As we have seen, the doctrine of justification by faith is a shorthand way of referring to the fact that God freely offers us, as a gift, redemption through the death and resurrection of Jesus Christ. It is clearly presupposed that we are incapable of redeeming ourselves. That which we could never achieve is offered to us as a gift by God. Fallen and rebellious humanity is utterly impotent to come unaided to the saving knowledge of God for which we were created. It is not a question of asking how we shall reconcile ourselves to God, but rather of receiving the reconciliation God has accomplished and is still accomplishing, in order that a new relationship may result. One of the more humbling aspects of the doctrine of justification is the insight that we contribute little to our own justification apart from accepting all that has already been done on our behalf.

3. As "judge over all other doctrines" (Luther), the doctrine of justification allows us to give a provisional definition of the limits of the Christian faith. We have already seen how the doctrine of justification allows us to define the saving work of God in Jesus Christ as standing at the heart of the Christian faith—but the doctrine of justification by faith also allows us to clarify the limits of that faith. How this may be done is of particular interest in relation to a perennial difficulty—the problem of defining heresy, and of distinguishing this from simple unbelief.

The problem of defining heresy has confronted the church from the earliest of times. If the distinctive essence of Christianity consists in the fact that God has redeemed us through Jesus Christ, it must follow that the Christian understanding of God, Jesus Christ, and humanity be consistent with this understanding of redemption. Thus the Christian understanding of God must be such that he can effect the redemption of humanity through Christ; the Christian understanding of humanity must be such that redemption is both possible and genuine. In other words, it is essential that the Christian understanding of God, Christ, and humanity be *consistent with* the doctrine of justification by faith. Let us develop this point.

First, let us note that the rejection or denial of the principle that God has redeemed us through Jesus Christ is nothing less than the rejection of Christianity itself. In other words, to deny that God has redeemed us through Jesus Christ is to deny the most fundamental truth claim the Christian faith dares to make. This isn't heresy—it is simply unbelief, a flat rejection of what Christianity has to say. In the early fifth century, the theologian Vincent of Lérins developed a test to determine whether something was authentically Christian or not—the so-called "Vincentian Canon."[11] According to Vincent, it was necessary to ask three crucial questions before deciding whether something was authentically Christian. First, was it believed everywhere? If there was a significant section of the Christian church that refused to accept a certain doctrine, it could not be regarded as authentic. Second, was it always believed? If it was a recent innovation, there were excellent reasons for questioning its authenticity. Third, was it believed by everyone? In other words, did the doctrine command widespread support among ordinary believers? Once more, the authenticity of any doctrine only believed by a small section of the Christian church down through the ages had to be challenged. Yet it is obvious that the basic principle encapsulated in the doctrine of justification satisfies all three conditions. The belief that God has redeemed humanity through Jesus Christ is probably the most central and characteristic feature of the Christian faith down through the ages—and to deny this is to step outside the limits of the Christian faith. The distinction between what is Christian and what is not lies in whether this doctrine is accepted: the distinction between what is orthodox and what is heretical, however, lies in how this doctrine, once conceded and accepted, is understood.

Heresy arises through accepting the basic principle but interpreting its terms in such a way that internal inconsistency results. In other words, the principle is granted, but it is inadequately understood: (1) It is interpreted in such a way that Christ cannot effect the redemption of humanity; and (2) it is interpreted in such a way that humanity—the object of justification—cannot be justified, properly speaking. Let us examine each of these possibilities.

Who is the redeemer? The answer given to this question must be able to account for the uniqueness of his office and for his ability to mediate between God and humanity. There must therefore be an essential similarity between Christ and ourselves if he is to be able to mediate between us and God, and yet at the same time there must be something fundamentally different about him—every human being is not, after all, a redeemer! Heresy can arise simply by failing to uphold these two points simultaneously, so that the affirmation of one amounts to the denial of the other. If the *difference* of Jesus Christ from us is emphasized without maintaining his essential similarity to us, his ability to reconcile us to God is lost, in that he no longer has a point of contact with those whom he is supposed to redeem. On the other hand, if his *similarity* to us is emphasized, without acknowledging that in at least one respect he is fundamentally different, then the redeemer himself requires redemption! If the redeemer is treated as being similar in every respect to us, he must be acknowledged to share our need for redemption. Therefore *either* all of us are actually redeemers, to a greater or lesser extent, or else the redeemer cannot redeem!

Two ways of approaching this may be noted. In the patristic period, two fundamental assumptions governed thinking on the redemption of mankind in Christ. First, only God can save. Unless Jesus Christ *is* God in some sense of the word, redemption is impossible. Second, "the unassumed is the unhealed."[12] In other words, if human nature is to be redeemed, it is essential that the redeemer (God) comes into contact with what is to be redeemed (human nature). Therefore, the patristic period was virtually unanimous in declaring that Jesus Christ, as the redeemer of mankind, had to be both God and man. In the modern period, however, the personalist philosophies, noted earlier, have laid emphasis on the need for a personal encounter of the reconciler (God) with those who are to be reconciled to him. God must meet us in a personal manner within history—in other words, he must meet us as a person. Once more, the traditional "two-natures" doctrine proves to preserve a crucial insight—that God meets us where we are through Jesus Christ. If it is not God who meets us in Jesus Christ, no reconciliation to God is possible. And if Jesus Christ is not a human being like us, the personal point of contact with us is lost.

It will be obvious that the doctrine of justification by faith requires that Jesus Christ shares our common humanity, except our need for redemption. After all, Christianity has always insisted that Jesus is a solution to the human dilemma, rather than part of the problem! Traditional Christianity has upheld this crucial insight by insisting that Jesus Christ is at one and the same time both God and man. It would be much simpler to suggest that Jesus was just God, or just man—but if we are to uphold the possibility and actuality of our justification, it is necessary to insist that they are both true. From the above discussion, it will be obvious that two heresies may arise when, though the principle of redemption through Christ is upheld, the person of Christ is interpreted in such a way that this redemption becomes impossible. On the one hand, Jesus Christ loses his point of contact with those he is meant to redeem—this heresy is generally known as *Docetism*.[13] On the other, he loses his essential dissimilarity from those whom he came to redeem, and comes to be treated simply as a particularly enlightened human being—a heresy generally known as *Ebionitism*.[14]

Who are the redeemed? The answer to this question must be capable of explaining why redemption is necessary from outside humanity itself—in other words, why we cannot redeem ourselves. The doctrine of justification affirms that we cannot *achieve* redemption, but that if someone else obtains that redemption for us we are in a position to *receive*. The object of redemption—we, ourselves—must both require redemption and be capable of accepting that redemption when it is offered to us. These two aspects of the question must be maintained at one and the same time, just like the humanity and divinity of Christ. If our need for redemption is granted, yet our impotence to redeem ourselves is denied, the conclusion follows that we would be the agents of our own redemption. This is not necessarily to say that each individual could redeem himself, but rather to suggest that individual A could redeem B, and individual B could redeem A. Reconciliation could then be effected by at least some individuals, if not by all, to varying degrees—which immediately contradicts the principle of redemption through Jesus Christ alone. And if our impotence to accept redemption, once it is offered to us, is denied, that redemption again becomes an impossibility. Broadly speaking, these two positions correspond to the Pelagian and the Manichaean heresies discussed in chapter 3.

The four positions we have just outlined are to be rejected as inadequate as much as false, in that they maintain the central principle of the doctrine of justification by faith—that we are redeemed through Christ alone—while interpreting its terms in such a way that inconsistency results. It is in this sense that the doctrine of justification by faith defines both the center and the limits of the Christian faith. It defines the center of the Christian faith as the gratuitous redemptive activity of God in Jesus Christ. It defines the limits of the Christian faith by regulating the interpretation of that redemptive activity. To bring this point out, let us develop a geometrical analogy.

The area of authentically *Christian* teaching on man and Christ can be compared with a square or rectangle, whose diagonals intersect at the center: the saving work of God in

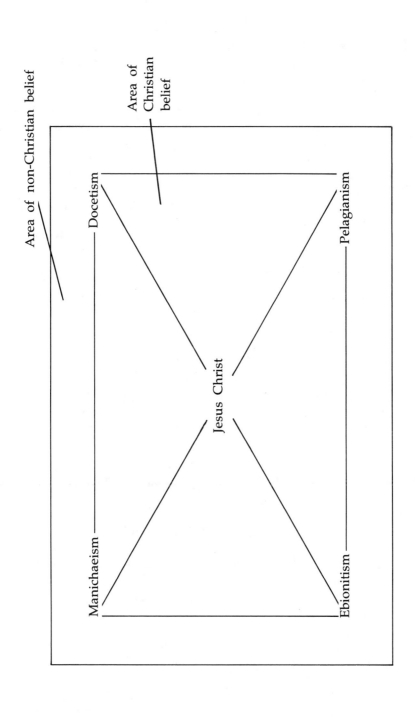

Area of non-Christian belief

Area of Christian belief

Docetism

Pelagianism

Manichaeism

Jesus Christ

Ebionitism

Jesus Christ. The limits of the Christian faith are defined by the four corners of that figure, corresponding to the Docetic and Ebionite heresies at the ends of one diagonal, and the Pelagian and Manichaean heresies at the end of the other. The area encompassed within that figure may be regarded as authentically Christian, in that redemption through Christ is asserted to be both *necessary* and *possible* in the terms stated.

The four heresies described above may be regarded as the four natural heresies of the Christian faith, each of which arises through an inadequate interpretation of the doctrine of justification by faith. It is no accident that these were by far the most important heresies to be debated in the early church, just as it is no accident that all four, under different names, are still encountered in the modern period. The doctrine of justification by faith gives us a way of demonstrating how these views arise, as well as an important means of dealing with them by helping us define both the center and the limits of the Christian faith.

On the basis of the above discussion, it will be clear that the doctrine of justification by faith provides an important method of ensuring the connection and continuity between Christian preaching and Christian theology. It provides a valuable cluster of checks and balances to ensure that theological speculation never gets out of hand but remains wedded to the creative saving encounter of God with humanity through Jesus Christ. Theology thus remains grounded in the Christian experience of redemption, and worship of Christ as redeemer and Lord.

FOR FURTHER READING

G. C. Berkouwer. *Faith and Justification*. Grand Rapids: Eerdmans, 1954.

Gerhard O. Forde. *Justification by Faith—A Matter of Death and Life*. Philadelphia: Fortress, 1982.

————. "Christian Life." In Carl E. Braaten and Robert W. Jenson, eds., *Christian Dogmatics*. 2 vols. Philadelphia: Fortress, 1982. 2:395–469.

Hans Küng. *Justification: The Doctrine of Karl Barth and a Catholic Reflection*. 2nd ed. Philadelphia: Westminster, 1981.

Alister E. McGrath. "The Article by which the Church stands or falls." *Evangelical Quarterly* 58/3 (1986): 207–28.

Peter Toon. *Justification and Sanctification.* Westchester, Ill.: Crossway, 1983.

NOTES

PREFACE

[1] *Iustitia Dei: A History of the Christian Doctrine of Justification*, 2 vols. (Cambridge: Cambridge University Press, 1986).

[2] Initially, the present work was modeled on Gerhard Müller's excellent college textbook *Die Rechfertigungslehre: Geschichte und Probleme* (Gütersloh: Mohn, 1977), but it soon became apparent that modifications to this model were necessary.

CHAPTER 1: INTRODUCTION

[1] Paul Tillich, "The Protestant Message and the Man of Today," in *The Protestant Era* (Chicago: University of Chicago Press, 1948), 196–98.

[2] C. S. Lewis, *God in the Dock* (Grand Rapids: Eerdmans, 1970), 96.

[3] For a discussion of the point at issue in relation to the Christological doctrines, see Alister E. McGrath, *Understanding Jesus: Who Jesus Christ Is and Why He Matters* (Grand Rapids: Zondervan, 1987), 29–36.

[4] David A. Shank, "Towards an Understanding of Christian Conversion," *Mission Focus* 5 (1976): 5. See further Harvie M. Conn, *Eternal Word and Changing Worlds: Theology, Anthropology and Mission in Trialogue* (Grand Rapids: Zondervan, 1984), for a stimulating analysis.

CHAPTER 2: THE BIBLICAL FOUNDATION

[1] For an analysis of the problem, see Alister E. McGrath, *Iustitia Dei: A History of the Christian Doctrine of Justification*, 2 vols. (Cambridge: Cambridge University Press, 1986), 1: 4–16.

[2] The full implications of the Hebrew idea of "righteousness" have probably only been fully realized since the publication of H. Cremer, *Die paulinische Rechtfertigungslehre im Zusammenhang ihrer geschichtlichen Voraussetzungen* (Gütersloh, 1899) ["The Pauline Doctrine of Justification in the Context of Its Historical Presuppositions"]. For a

summary of Cremer's views, see Walther Eichrodt, *Theology of the Old Testament*, 2 vols. (Philadelphia: Westminster, 1975), 1: 240–41.

[3] See especially Ernst Käsemann, *Commentary on Romans* (Grand Rapids: Eerdmans, 1980).

[4] This point is argued by E. P. Sanders, *Paul and Palestinian Judaism* (Philadelphia: Fortress, 1977), and more recently in his *Paul, The Law and the Jewish People* (Philadelphia: Fortress, 1983). For a response to Sanders' views, see W. D. Davies, *Paul and Rabbinic Judaism*, 2nd ed. (Philadelphia: Fortress, 1980).

CHAPTER 3: AUGUSTINE AND THE PELAGIAN CONTROVERSY

[1] For details, see Peter Brown, *Augustine of Hippo: A Biography* (Berkeley: University of California Press, 1967), 101–14.

[2] See Alister E. McGrath, *Iustitia Dei: A History of the Christian Doctrine of Justification*, 2 vols. (Cambridge: Cambridge University Press, 1986), 1: 17–23.

[3] For the course of the controversy, see Brown, *Augustine of Hippo*, 340–735.

CHAPTER 4: THE REFORMATION

[1] For details of the medieval and Reformation debates, see Alister E. McGrath, *Iustitia Dei: A History of the Christian Doctrine of Justification*, 2 vols. (Cambridge: Cambridge University Press, 1986), 1: 37–187.

[2] For details of this school, see Alister E. McGrath, *The Intellectual Origins of the European Reformation* (New York: Basil Blackwell, 1987), 69–85.

[3] For details see Alister E. McGrath, *Luther's Theology of the Cross: Martin Luther's Theological Breakthrough* (New York: Basil Blackwell, 1985), 53–63; 85–92.

[4] *Luther's Works*, 54 vols. (Philadelphia: Muhlenberg, 1956–76), 34: 336–38; McGrath, *Luther's Theology of the Cross*, 95–98.

[5] As quoted in Charles W. Carter, ed., *A Contemporary Wesleyan Theology* (Grand Rapids: Zondervan, 1983), 344.

[6] See McGrath, *Iustitia Dei*, 2: 20–32, for details.

[7] See McGrath, *Iustitia Dei*, 2: 32–39, for a discussion.

[8]John Calvin, *Institutes of the Christian Religion*, trans. Henry Beveridge, 2 vols. (Grand Rapids: Eerdmans, 1975), 2: 99.

CHAPTER 5: DENOMINATIONAL DIFFERENCES

[1]For the reasons why, see Alister E. McGrath, *Iustitia Dei: A History of the Christian Doctrine of Justification*, 2 vols. (Cambridge: Cambridge University Press, 1986), 1: 2–4.

[2]For a detailed analysis, see ibid., 2: 44–51.

[3]See ibid., 51–53, for the five main points of divergence.

[4]John Wesley, *Sermons on Several Occasions* (London: Epworth, 1944), 174.

[5]Heidelberg Catechism, Q.60, in Arthur C. Cochrane, *Reformed Confessions of the 16th Century* (Philadelphia: Westminster, 1966), 315. Questions 61–64 (pp. 315–16) are also relevant to this discussion.

[6]The term often used in connection with discussions of the nature of justifying righteousness is *the formal cause of justification*—in other words, the *immediate* cause of justification. Although it is possible to distinguish various causes of our justification (for example, the grace of God, the merit of Christ, and so forth), the Protestant–Roman-Catholic debate has tended to center on the immediate (that is, formal) cause of justification. For the Protestant, the formal cause of justification is imputed righteousness; for the Roman Catholic, it is inherent righteousness.

An interesting theology of justification, which attempts to mediate between the Roman Catholic and Protestant positions, is known as *double justification*. This view, associated with Girolamo Seripando at the Council of Trent and several theologians of the Church of England in the later seventeenth century, holds that there is a double or two-fold formal cause of justification: the imputed righteousness of Christ and inherent righteousness. In practice, this doctrine has had little influence and is of purely historical interest.

[7]For the development of this distinction and its significance, see McGrath, *Iustitia Dei*, 1: 109–19; 2: 80–9 (esp. 83–89).

[8]For the doctrines of justification associated with the Enlightenment, see McGrath, *Iustitia Dei*, 2: 136–48.

CHAPTER 6: THE EXISTENTIAL DIMENSION

[1] See, e.g., James O. Buswell, III, "Contextualization: Theory, Tradition and Method," in David J. Hesselgrave, ed., *Theology and Mission* (Grand Rapids: Baker, 1978), 93–99; Bruce J. Nichols, *Contextualization: A Theology of Gospel and Culture* (Downers Grove: InterVarsity, 1979).

[2] See David E. Roberts, *Existentialism and Religious Belief* (New York: Oxford University Press, 1959).

[3] Thus Romans 8:4, which states that believers do not live according to the flesh, but according to the Spirit: the New International Version translates, . . . "do not live according to the sinful nature, but according to the Spirit," correctly identifying "flesh" with "sinful nature."

CHAPTER 7: THE PERSONAL DIMENSION

[1] Such as C. S. Lewis; see his *Letters to Malcolm: Chiefly on Prayer* (New York: Harcourt Brace Jovanovich, 1955), 63–65. At this point, we must note a difficulty in terminology. The term "person" is used in two slightly different senses in connection with the doctrine of God: in one sense, God is one person; in another, he is three persons. For a demonstration that the trinitarian doctrine of God as *three* persons is implicitly contained in the idea of a personal God, see Alister McGrath, *Understanding the Trinity* (Grand Rapids: Zondervan, 1988).

[2] His most influential work is *I and Thou*, which should be read in the translation by Walter Kaufmann (New York: Scribner, 1970).

[3] For example, in the field of Christology: see Alister E. McGrath, *The Making of Modern German Christology: From the Enlightenment to Pannenberg* (New York: Basil Blackwell, 1986), 101–3.

[4] Buber, *I and Thou*, 56.

[5] C. S. Lewis, *The Weight of Glory* (New York: Macmillan, 1949), 8.

[6] Evelyn Waugh, *Brideshead Revisited* (New York: Dell, 1968), 288.

CHAPTER 8: THE ETHICAL DIMENSION

[1] The most famous exposition of the political relevance of Barth's thought remains Friedrich-Wilhelm Marquardt, *Theologie und Sozialismus: Das Beispiel Karl Barths* [Theology and Socialism: The Example of Karl Barth], 3rd ed. (Munich: Kaiser Verlag, 1985).

[2]The most distinguished and reliable discussion of this question may be found in Helmut Thielicke, *Theological Ethics*, 3 vols. (Grand Rapids: Eerdmans, 1978), vol. 1, esp. pp. 27–38.

[3]German-speaking theologians like to play with the words *Gabe* ("gift") and *Aufgabe* ("task"). Another relevant play on words is between *Angebot* ("invitation") and *Gebot* ("commandment"). Unfortunately, this word-play can't be translated into English!

[4]William Romaine, *A Method for Preventing the Frequency of Robbers and Murders* (London, 1770), 17.

[5]Reinhold Niebuhr, *Moral Man and Immoral Society* (New York: Scribner, 1932), 44.

[6]Reinhold Niebuhr, *The Nature and Destiny of Man*, 2 vols. (New York: Scribner, 1941–43), 2: 82.

CHAPTER 9: CONCLUSION

[1]It is interesting to note the close connection in Luther's thought between the doctrine of justification by faith and the "theology of the cross." See Alister E. McGrath, *Luther's Theology of the Cross: Martin Luther's Theological Breakthrough* (New York: Basil Blackwell, 1985), 149–751, esp. 153–61.

APPENDIX

[1]For a more detailed discussion of this question see Alister E. McGrath, *Understanding Jesus: Who Jesus Christ Is and Why He Matters* (Grand Rapids: Zondervan, 1987).

[2]For the relationship between Christology and soteriology, see Alister E. McGrath, "Christology and Soteriology: A Response to Wolfhart Pannenberg's Critique of the Soteriological Approach to Christology," *Theologische Zeitschrift* 42/3 (1986): 222–36.

[3]For a brief discussion of these terms, see McGrath, *Understanding Jesus*, 123–36.

[4]For the reasons underlying this selection, see Alister E. McGrath, *Iustitia Dei: A History of the Christian Doctrine of Justification*, 2 vols. (Cambridge: Cambridge University Press, 1986).

[5]See Alister E. McGrath, "The Article by which the Church stands or falls," *Evangelical Quarterly* 58/3 (1986): 207–28.

[6] For a detailed study of this theme, see Alister McGrath, *The Mystery of the Cross* (Grand Rapids: Zondervan, 1988). See also Walter von Loewenich, *Luther's Theology of the Cross* (Minneapolis: Augsburg, 1976), 17–24.

[7] Karl Barth, *Church Dogmatics* (Edinburgh: T. & T. Clark, 1956), IV/1, 518.

[8] For a fuller discussion, see Alister E. McGrath, "Justification and Christology: The Axiomatic Correlation between the Proclaimed Christ and the Historical Jesus," *Modern Theology* 1/1 (1984): 45–54.

[9] For further discussion of what follows, see Alister E. McGrath, "Reformation to Enlightenment," in P. D. L. Avis, ed., *The History of Christian Theology I: The Science of Theology* (Grand Rapids: Eerdmans, 1986), 105–229, esp. 154–60.

[10] Lausanne Covenant, para. 10.

[11] This is often stated as "what has been believed everywhere, always and by everyone" (*quod ubique, quod semper, quod ab omnibus creditum est*).

[12] Gregory of Nazianzen, *Epistle* 101. See further M. F. Wiles, "The Unassumed Is the Unhealed," *Religious Studies* 4 (1968): 47–56.

[13] From the Greek word meaning "to appear." Docetism held that Christ's humanity and sufferings were apparent, rather than real. In other words, Jesus Christ was God disguised as a human being: God never knew at first hand what it was like to be human.

[14] The name derives from a small sect of Jewish Christians in the first two centuries, who held that Jesus Christ was the human son of Mary and Joseph, singled out for special favor by God. In no meaningful sense of the word could he be said to *be* God.

BIBLIOGRAPHY

The articles and books listed below will enable the reader to develop some of the historical and theological themes encountered during the course of this work. It is not intended to be exhaustive, but simply to allow the reader to take further any ideas that have been found stimulating in the present work.

Achtemeier, E. R. "Righteousness in the Old Testament." In *Interpreter's Dictionary of the Bible*. Nashville: Abingdon, 1962. 4:80–85.

Atkinson, J. "Justification by Faith: A Truth for Our Times." In David Field, ed., *Here We Stand: Justification by Faith Today*. London: Hodder & Stoughton, 1986. 57–83.

Berkouwer, G. C. *Faith and Justification*. Grand Rapids: Eerdmans, 1954.

Bray, G. "Justification and the Eastern Orthodox Churches." In David Field, ed., *Here We Stand: Justification by Faith Today*. London: Hodder & Stoughton, 1986. 103–19.

Brown, C. et al. "Righteousness, Justification." In *New International Dictionary of New Testament Theology*. Grand Rapids: Zondervan, 1976. 3:352–76. This work has an excellent bibliography.

Forde, Gerhard O. *Justification by Faith—A Matter of Death and Life*. Philadelphia: Fortress, 1982.

———. "Christian Life." In Carl E. Braaten and Robert W. Jenson, eds., *Christian Dogmatics*. 2 vols. Philadelphia: Fortress, 1982. 2:395–469.

Käsemann, E. "The 'Righteousness of God' in Paul." In *New Testament Questions of Today*. Philadelphia: Fortress, 1969. 168–82.

———. *Commentary on Romans*. Grand Rapids: Eerdmans, 1980.

Küng, H. *Justification: The Doctrine of Karl Barth and a Catholic Reflection*. 2nd ed. Philadelphia: Westminster, 1981.

Lampe, G. W. H., ed. *The Doctrine of Justification by Faith*. London: Mowbrays, 1954.

McGrath, A. E. "The Anti-Pelagian Structure of 'Nominalist' Doctrines of Justification." *Ephemerides Theologicae Lovanienses* 57 (1981): 107–19.

————. "'Augustinianism'? A Critical Assessment of the So-called 'Mediaeval Augustinian Tradition' on Justification." *Augustiniana* 31 (1981): 247–67.

————. "Justification: Barth, Trent and Küng." *Scottish Journal of Theology* 34 (1981): 517–29.

————. "Justice and Justification. Semantic and Juristic Aspects of the Christian Doctrine of Justification." *Scottish Journal of Theology* 35 (1982): 403–18.

————. "Humanist Elements in the Early Reformed Doctrine of Justification." *Archiv für Reformationsgeschichte* 73 (1982): 5–20.

————. "Forerunners of the Reformation? A Critical Examination of the Evidence for Precursors of the Reformation Doctrines of Justification." *Harvard Theological Review* 75 (1982): 219–42.

————. "'The Righteousness of God' from Augustine to Luther." *Studia Theologica* 36 (1982): 63–78.

————. "Mira et nova diffinitio iustitiae. Luther and Scholastic Doctrines of Justification." *Archiv für Reformationsgeschichte* 74 (1982): 37–60.

————. "John Henry Newman's 'Lectures on Justification.' The High Church Interpretation of Luther." *The Churchman* 97 (1983): 112–22.

————. "Karl Barth and the *articulus iustificationis*. The Significance of His Critique of Ernst Wolf within the Context of His Theological Method." *Theologische Zeitschrift* 39 (1983): 349–61.

————. "Justification and Christology. The Axiomatic Correlation between the Proclaimed Christ and the Historical Jesus." *Modern Theology* 1 (1984–85): 45–54.

————. "ARCIC II and Justification. Some Difficulties and Obscurities relating to Anglican and Roman Catholic Teaching on Justification." *Anvil* 1 (1984): 27–42.

————. "The Emergence of the Anglican Tradition on Justification 1600–1700." *The Churchman* 98 (1984): 28–43.

————. "Justification in Earlier Evangelicalism." *The Churchman* 97 (1983): 217–28.

————. "The Influence of Aristotelian Physics upon St Thomas Aquinas' Discussion of the 'Processus Iustificationis.'" *Recherches de théologie ancienne et médiévale* 51 (1984): 223–39.

————. *Luther's Theology of the Cross: Martin Luther's Theological Breakthrough*. New York: Basil Blackwell, 1985.

————. "The Moral Theory of the Atonement. An Historical and Theological Critique." *Scottish Journal of Theology* 38 (1985): 205–20.

————. "The Article by which the Church Stands or Falls." *Evangelical Quarterly* 58 (1986): 207–28.

————. "Christology and Soteriology. A Response to Wolfhart Pannenberg's Critique of the Soteriological Approach to Christology." *Theologische Zeitschrift* 42 (1986): 222–36.

————. *Iustitia Dei: A History of the Christian Doctrine of Justification.* 2 vols. Cambridge: Cambridge University Press, 1986.

Packer, J. I. "Justification in Protestant Theology." In David Field, ed., *Here We Stand: Justification by Faith Today.* London: Hodder & Stoughton, 1986. 84–102.

Przybylski, B. *Righteousness in Matthew and His World of Thought.* Cambridge: Cambridge University Press, 1980.

Reumann, J. *Righteousness in the New Testament.* Grand Rapids: Eerdmans, 1983.

Stendahl, K. "The Apostle Paul and the Introspective Conscience of the West." In *Paul among Jews and Gentiles.* Philadelphia: Fortress, 1976. 78–96.

Thielicke, H. *Theological Ethics.* 3 vols. Grand Rapids: Eerdmans, 1978.

Tiller, John. "Justification by Faith and the Sacraments." In Gavin Reid, ed., *The Great Acquittal: Justification by Faith and Current Christian Thought.* London: Fount, 1980. 38–61.

Toon, P. *Justification and Sanctification.* Westchester, Ill.: Crossway, 1983.

Wright, T. "Justification: The Biblical Basis and Its Relevance for Contemporary Evangelicalism." In Gavin Reid, ed., *The Great Acquittal: Justification by Faith and Current Christian Thought.* London: Fount, 1980. 12–37.

Yarnold, E. J. *The Second Gift: A Study of Grace.* London: St Paul Publications, 1974.

Ziesler, J. A. *The Meaning of Righteousness in Paul.* Cambridge: Cambridge University Press, 1972.

INDEX